One Day
You Will Understand

Trusting God When Life Doesn't Make Sense

Adrian Ghiduc

One Day You Will Understand

Trusting God When Life Doesn't Make Sense

© 2020 by Adrian Ghiduc

Scripture quotations marked (BSB) are taken from The Holy Bible, Berean Study Bible, Copyright ©2016, 2018 by Bible Hub. Used by Permission. All Rights Reserved Worldwide.

Scripture quotations marked (ESV) are taken from the Holy Bible, English Standard Version. ESV® Text Edition: 2016. Copyright © 2001 by Crossway Bibles, a publishing ministry of Good News Publishers.

Scripture quotations marked (GNT) are taken from the Good News Translation (GNT) Copyright © 1992 by American Bible Society.

Scripture quotations marked (KJV) are taken from the Holy Bible, King James Version, Public domain.

Scripture quotations marked (MSG) are taken from The Message (MSG). Copyright © 1993, 2002, 2018 by Eugene H. Peterson.

Scripture quotations marked (NASB) are taken from the New American Standard Bible (NASB). Copyright © 1960, 1962, 1963, 1968, 1971, 1972, 1973, 1975, 1977, 1995 by The Lockman Foundation.

Scripture quotations marked (NIV) are taken from the Holy Bible, New International Version®, NIV® Copyright ©1973, 1978, 1984, 2011 by Biblica, Inc.® Used by permission. All rights reserved worldwide.

Scripture quotations marked (NJB) are taken from the Jerusalem Bible. Copyright © 1966, 1967, 1968 by Darton, Longmand & Todd LTD and Doubleday and Co. Inc. All rights reserved.

Scripture quotations marked (NLT) are taken from the Holy Bible, New Living Translation, copyright © 1996, 2004, 2015 by Tyndale House Foundation. Used by permission of Tyndale House Publishers, Inc., Carol Stream, Illinois 60188. All rights reserved.

Scripture quotations marked (TLB) are taken from The Living Bible copyright © 1971 by Tyndale House Foundation. Used by permission of Tyndale House Publishers Inc., Carol Stream, Illinois 60188. All rights reserved.

Interior Text Formatting: affordablechristianediting.com

Cover Design: Jeff Zdrentan

Printed and Bound in the United States

Dedication

To my wife Oana
and to my son Edison,
my precious treasures.

Table of Contents

Introduction

ONE MORNING, while I was washing my face, I felt as though I had wiped off a thick covering layer. When I looked in the mirror, I started to see beyond the image I usually saw. What I was seeing was still me, but I began to see my weaknesses, disadvantages, and lacks with an unusual clarity. I felt as though I was looking through a window at an image on the other side. At first, some of the images began as mere flashes, but then snapshots increasingly dominated my physical image in the mirror.

Odd, I thought. *Nothing like that has ever happened to me before.*

I was a pastor; I knew the Bible fairly well, and I lived a positive life. Now a new voice was making itself heard louder and louder in the chamber of my mind. That voice began to replay the same scenarios for months on end. The conversation I did not want to address concerned the disadvantages I felt I had in comparison to others, the weaknesses I recognized in certain areas of my life, the mistakes of the past that seemed recent, all the unanswered prayers, the betrayals experienced, and even more.

The negative thoughts and arguments began to patrol my

mind like a closed maze, bringing clouds of doubt and sorrow on the horizon. These rapidly approaching clouds were coming to swallow up my enthusiasm and joy of living.

~

Have you experienced moments like these when the weaknesses and disadvantages crowded your mind and began to bring heaviness? Do you remember the voice that kept repeating that you are not at the same level as those around you? Have you ever heard the echo of that voice saying that your lack of intellectual and physical ability puts you behind in the line? Do you feel you are not good enough? Has the idea that God does not answer your prayers because He does not care about you ever strolled through your mind? Have you ever heard the accusatory voice of past mistakes making you feel unworthy?

After a few years, I decided I had to do something about the weaknesses, the negative dialogue, the accusations, and the disadvantages that were devouring the perimeter of my life's joy. I started to pray to seek answers in order to replace them with qualities or at least frame them elsewhere in my life.

I noticed that some people simply do not admit the fact that they have disadvantages, weaknesses, and mistakes. They live their lives in a sort of denial. On the other hand, in order to have a pleasant life before them for those around them and before God, some focus on fixing these negatives and take steps to remove them from their lives at all costs. They understand that their weaknesses and disadvantages cause them to feel unloved and unappreciated.

Certainly, various aspects in our lives need to be changed

because they bear the mark of sin or are present because we went against God's principles. However, God has left some weaknesses and disadvantages in our lives to fulfill a specific purpose. Good judgment is needed to differentiate between what must be changed and what must be accepted.

The purpose of this book is to highlight how God has left certain weaknesses and disadvantages in our life in order for His power to manifest through them. Even if they are painful and we do not understand why they exist, they have a role in His divine plan.

The apostle Paul also had a weakness, a pain that he prayed for the Lord to remove. But God's answer to his plea was: *"My grace is sufficient for you, for my power is made perfect in weakness."*[1]

Elsewhere the apostle writes, *"But we have this treasure in jars of clay to show that this all-surpassing power is from God and not from us."*[2]

The Almighty Designer allows weaknesses and disadvantages in our lives—not so that they might disqualify us but because they are the cracks through which His power manifests within us and through us. God's point of view is often different than what we have in mind. He does not choose the best and the most talented; rather, He chooses the weak instruments characterized by disadvantages and mistakes so that His power may manifest through them. The Almighty does not want the clay to brag about his or her accomplishments; all the glory needs to be ascribed to Him.

We often have the impression that God is upset with us

because of our weaknesses, and many times, we fervently work on fixing them. However, if the weaknesses are His design to demonstrate His power, then we must realize that we are working against His plans.

This book contains examples and explanations for those who have doubts, scars and weaknesses and do not understand these roles in God's plan. The book is addressed to those who are fighting the battles of negative mental dialogue, for those who have made mistakes and want to be found by divine grace, and for those who do not understand why God doesn't answer their prayers.

If you see these struggles when you look at your life in the mirror, then this book is for you.

CHAPTER ONE

Beyond Expectations

"Whatever it is you're seeking won't come in the form you're expecting."

> – Haruki Marukami

"The Lord has done this for me," she said. "In these days he has shown his favor and taken away my disgrace among the people." — Luke 1:25 (NIV)

AFTER OUR son, Edison was born, I often went to the pediatrician with him for routine checkups.

I still remember his six-month checkup. After the doctor checked him as usual, she looked at us and said, "There is nothing to be worried about, but I want to refer you to a specialist to see him. Something seems unusual about his head."

My eyes widened. Suddenly, huge question marks appeared in my mind.

After waiting some time for an appointment, I nervously walked with my son into the specialist's office. The specialist carefully examined him and then said, "I am not certain, but it seems that the bone plates covering his brain are fusing together prematurely. If this is the case, his brain will be unable to develop normally. I want you to make an appointment to return in three months so we can monitor his progress."

His words seemed like the thunder's announcing a great storm on the horizon. I could not believe what I was hearing. Edison was healthy, behaved normally, and did not exhibit any outward symptoms or problems. The doctor's words created a great sense of uneasiness in our souls. We felt as though a thick fog was setting on the horizon for our family.

I knew that such devastating news can shake up a family from every aspect. I started praying for Edison's health and to eliminate any illness so that he could develop in peace.

We returned to the doctor's office after three months. When we sat down for our consultation, four doctors filed into the room. My heart began to beat harder in my chest. The doctor who had first examined Edison introduced us to a surgeon and two other specialists.

The four doctors felt Edison's cranial plates and took measurements. After consulting together, we were told, "It seems that the bone plates have fused together, and his brain will be unable to develop appropriately. If you touch here, you can feel what we feel."

I touched where the doctors indicated, and I felt something that, after their explanations, convinced me that our son could have serious problems.

"What do we do from here?"

The doctors continued, "If the plates are fused together, we will have to perform an intervention and separate them." The surgeon began to describe the process.

My imagination began to run wild as I tried to create quick visual images of the surgeons cutting and separating the fused cranial plates. The resulting visuals were horrific, shocking, and as a parent, struck fear in my heart. My heart was saying, *"This can't be done to Edison's little head."* An enormous internal storm stirred within me.

When my wife, Oana, and I left the hospital, we were upset, tearful and sorrowful. I was conducting an interior monologue with God. *Why God? Why did we reach such a state? I simply don't understand, and I don't want Edison to end up on the operating table. God, I beg You, help us!*

I was driving on the highway with my eyes full of tears and with a tornado stirring in my soul. Suddenly, I noticed a red car aggressively cutting into my lane on the highway and slowing down almost to a stop. Already upset, I was preparing to honk my horn and push the car out of the way if necessary. I felt so stricken in my spirit, the person's disrespectful driving simply bothered me. Suddenly, a bumper sticker on the red car caught my attention. When I looked more closely, I saw my answer in big letters:

Trust Me, I Am the Doctor [God]!

I could not believe what I was seeing and reading. In that moment, I understood in my soul that the driver aggressively cutting me off had a special message to remind me that God is the Supreme Doctor who heals. I quickly took out my phone to snap a picture to remind me of that message in my moments of doubt.

My wife and I prayed for Edison, and my extended family and the church family prayed corporately for him. After some time, we apprehensively took him for a CT scan. We were somewhat prepared to go through the storm showing on the horizon. What happened between the checkup with the four doctors and that scheduled CT scan—I don't know. What I do know is that the results came back showing that Edison was completely healthy! God, the Supreme Doctor, had worked beyond our expectations.

> *"Now to him who is able to do immeasurably more than all we ask or imagine, according to his power that is at work within us, to him be glory in the church and in Christ Jesus throughout all generations, for ever and ever! Amen."*[3]

God specializes in turning the most painful and disastrous of situations into huge blessings.

Perhaps you see financial obstacles, health problems or relationship problems rising up like waves on the horizon, but He is above the waves and works beyond your expectations. Perhaps you cannot see any way to solve a problem but know that He already has a solution prepared. God can do more than we ask for in prayer, or we can imagine because He has all the power on heaven and on earth. When you are going through moments of deep crisis, these truths will hold outstanding weight.

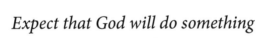

Expect that God will do something outstanding for you!

Luke the doctor describes the lives of two young people who were married in the early days of the New Testament. He describes their hopes, their struggles, the pain of disagreement, waiting in faith, the marks of a lack of faith, and the joys that crossed their paths in life. They came from very good families, and their relatives speculated that the young couple would have a bright future opening up ahead. "They will certainly be a model family who will be successful in life in all aspects."

Elizabeth had descended from the lineage of the high priest Aaron, the brother of Moses—a lineage that set her apart from other young ladies of her time. In her genes, she had the qualities of a future refined lady. Zechariah, who also descended from a family of priests, had studied at the seminary of that day and had subsequently entered into the priesthood.

In that society, religious structures were eminently important, and those around saw this couple as people who would become part of the cream of society. The Bible describes the two as being blameless before God, people who obeyed all of God's commandments and rules.[4]

The picture of the couple's life that the writer paints in words is a marvelous spiritual landscape. The two were simply full of praise but, while the painter's hand created the image, he placed a black stain in the middle. This dark stain in their lives caused much pain and ate at their souls: Elizabeth was infertile, unable to bear children.

During that time, great social pressure was placed on women who were unable to bear children. Their stigma became the talk and their disgrace as people believed they were being punished by God for hidden sins. No doubt Elizabeth felt like an unfulfilled woman and dealt with enough sorrow in her own family life; she didn't need the talk of her friends and neighbors to add to her sorrow.

I imagine as the two got older and no children came along, the whispered words and glares of those they knew became even more cutting and judgmental. When Elizabeth was walking through the village or went to get water from the well, women likely cast poisonous darts from behind their fences that were meant to pierce her soul and further humiliate her. *Certainly, the priest and priestess are hiding their sin. It is in vain that they are considered blameless. Heaven is against them, and that is why they have no children.*

Zechariah often found Elizabeth crying in her room because she was full of sorrow and felt unfulfilled. "Tell me, Zechariah. Why won't God give us children? What have we done wrong? We've obeyed all His laws and commandments. Haven't we done everything we could to abide by His will? Why? I want to hold a little child of my own in my arms. I promise that I will be the best mother in the world. I feel so alone! Why won't the Almighty do for me what He did for Samuel's mother Hannah who was also barren? When she prayed to God, He opened her womb, and she gave birth to multiple children. Just like her, I pray with my soul full of sorrow. Why did God give her children, but not me? Why is the heaven deaf and mute to all my prayers? You're a priest; tell me, explain!"

Even if Zechariah had no new answers and had had those conversations with her hundreds, maybe thousands of times, he hugged her lovingly each time.

With each passing year, Elisabeth's soul broke within her more and more, and she spiraled deeper and deeper into doubt. Zechariah didn't understand why the heavens were mute before their ardent prayers. He needed only one explanation to calm his grieving wife.

Likewise, many questions filtered through the priest's mind, and he would have liked to find a theological explanation for his wife's barrenness, or to find a way in life to correct the situation, or to accuse himself of being guilty for what was going on. Try as he might, he couldn't. He didn't know what else to say.

"All happy families are alike; every unhappy family is unhappy in its own way."[5]

Life is often like a beautifully colored painting, full of smiles and joy. However, in the center of this image, a black stain can sometimes appear, ruining the beauty of the image with its darkness. That stain can be an illness you have, distress that suddenly comes along bringing sorrow into your life, a child defeated by addiction, or the feeling of being misunderstood or feeling rejected by those around you. The dark stain on the painting of your life can be a broken relationship, a financial problem, misunderstandings at work, or the lack of funds for monthly expenses. We see in life sometimes a person, an event, or a season coming that transforms the joyful atmosphere to one of sorrow and pain.

Have you experienced such moments when a "dark stain" ruined the peace in your life? At that moment questions began to congregate at your mind's door—the way they had congregated at the door of Elizabeth's mind and now crowded her conscious and subconscious thoughts.

You feel lost in the maze of unanswered questions and cannot seem to find your way out. You use up considerable energy and time trying to discover why God allowed those details to happen in your life and fail to find any acceptable answers.

Why am I suffering? What good can come of this pain that I'm having? Why did my parent or this angel of a child pass so quickly into the other world? Why did I lose my job? Why is life not fair with me? Why must I go through this suffering that is consuming me? Why doesn't God intervene? Why did the Almighty not stop that situation from occurring?

We often find ourselves lost
in the maze of unanswered questions
that are consuming us, and we don't understand
why God does not intervene.

A Crisis of Faith

The inner pressure that Zechariah and Elizabeth experienced was partly caused by the pressure from their society. The public's opinion that they were being punished for offending God through hidden sin was in direct contrast to the truth: their lives were pure before the heaven.

Put yourself in their shoes. You do what is right in the eyes of God, while the religious culture accuses you of hidden sin and says, "That is why you do not have children."

Our religious mindsets, those frameworks in which we think, process and make judgments can so easily inflict pain in the lives of those who do not conform to our understanding of how things should be.[6]

I don't know if you've gone through moments when those around you have cast you in a negative light because of a religious or cultural mindset. This injustice that some experience is painful because people who judge others based on certain pre-established mindsets don't allow God to act and develop

His plan the way He wants. People often become mired in an obsolete paradigm, failing to accept that He can do new, different things or work in a way that goes beyond our thought criterion. The religious mindset has made victims of many among those who have ridden the wave raised by the Holy Spirit or who adjust the sails of their ships in the direction that the Holy Spirit's wind blows.

Tensions were rising in the couple's life and, due to spiritual pressure, they prayed for years for the heavens to solve their problem of infertility, but heaven remained unmoved to all of their requests. They served God faithfully, but still He did not respond to their ardent prayers.

This young couple did not know how to resolve the tensions and inner pain they experienced. Life launched projectiles at them from every direction, and their defense became like a spider web. Yet, Zechariah and Elizabeth continued to believe in the unchanging God who had promised that He had wonderful plans for His children.

When you are unable to reconcile your pain and prayers with God's silence to your situation for a long period of time, a crisis of faith often looms on the horizon. This battle of the soul becomes even more intense when you live a pure life and cannot explain in any way why the God you serve is indifferent to your ardent prayers when you present Him with your pain. If you live in sin, then you will blame yourself for the pain you are experiencing. However, if you live a pure life, not understanding things for a long period of time can shake your faith. In this season you are on God's workbench behind the scenes so He can process your faith and develop the good plans He has for you beyond what you see.

During that same time, the Enemy will bring questions filled with doubt toward God, and he will cause you ruminate on them to make you doubt His love and good plans. During that same difficult period sometimes, you will get the impression that if you could somehow understand what is going on behind God's curtain, you could minimize the pain and suffering and you might accept or resolve the situation.

The Olive Press

"Then Jesus went with them to a place called Gethsemane...."[7]

Gethsemane means "olive press" because the garden had a press for extracting oil from the olives. The process began with crushing the olives using a heavy rock shaped like a wheel that would compress the olives into a paste-like blend, which was placed in large cloth bags. The cloth sacks were then inserted in the olive press to be pressed again and causing the pure oil to drip out and be collected in jars.

The process of extracting the oil involved crushing. Were inanimate objects capable of feeling, the procedure would have been excruciating for the olives, but crushing was the only way to extract the oil. Great value was placed on the oil because of its varied uses, including healing, lighting the darkness, producing cosmetics, and anointing kings, priests and prophets.

Jesus's entry into the garden of Gethsemane, i.e., into the

"olive press," holds a separate symbolism. He entered into the crushing process as He endured the Roman soldiers' whips, the unfair accusations, crucifixion, being burdened with humanity's sins and dying. The blood flowed from His wounds the way that oil flowed from the crushed olives. His blood brought salvation for people; Christ became the "ointment" to heal our souls, and His presence sweetens even the most bitter of life's situations. Even His names *Christ* in the Greek and *Messiah* in the Hebrew mean "anointed one."

> *Yet it was the will of the LORD to crush him; he has put him to grief; when his soul makes an offering for guilt, he shall see his offspring; he shall prolong his days; the will of the LORD shall prosper in his hand. Out of the anguish of his soul he shall see and be satisfied; by his knowledge shall the righteous one, my servant, make many to be accounted righteous, and he shall bear their iniquities"* (Isaiah 53:10-11 ESV).

At some point each of us will go through the "olive press"—through our own personal Gethsemane. The pressure exerted will vary in intensity, but the common factor will be suffering. What we must remember in those moments is that the place of pain and suffering is not the place where everything ends; rather, it is the "press" through which He processes us into pure and valuable oil.

By personifying the olive, we can look at the process from its point of view: the crushing is painful, insufferable and useless. The olive is ready to scream at the person putting it through the press and desires to escape; however, the press is the only way to extract the precious oil. When going through the press of suffering, we must look beyond the great wheel causing crushing pain, and we must look at what we will become after the process is complete. We must see the oil that will be produced to bring healing to others' wounds. We must see, through faith, the aromatic oil that will bring joy to those going through life's sorrows. We must see the light the oil will provide to those who are going through the dark valleys of despair. As long as we do not look for an exit out of the press or allow sorrow to envelop us, the harder the crushing, the more useful we will become in the hands of God. We will become a refined and valuable oil.

Nelson Mandela said, "As I walked out the door toward that gate that would lead to my freedom, I knew if I didn't leave my bitterness and hatred behind, I'd still be in prison."[8]

"Count it all joy, my brothers, when you meet trials of various kinds, for you know that the testing of your faith produces steadfastness. And let steadfastness have its full effect, that you may be perfect and complete, lacking in nothing" (James 1:2-4 ESV).

"In this you rejoice, though now for a little while, if necessary, you have been grieved by various trials, so that the tested genuineness of your faith—more precious than gold that perishes though it is tested by fire—may be found to result in praise and glory and honor at the revelation of Jesus Christ" (1 Peter 1:6-7 ESV).

The trials and suffering you go through are the oil press God uses to process you into valuable oil.

Prayer

Zechariah and Elizabeth were able to resist pressure and social disgrace by praying to God to solve the situation. However, years passed and wrinkles appeared, but their problem still remained unsolved. They were getting older, and I can imagine Elizabeth telling her husband the following at the dinner table:

"Zechariah, we have prayed our whole lives for a child, but I have to tell you, I've reached the age when I am no longer biologically able to have children. What will we do now? Do we keep praying for a child or stop?"

I have also often asked myself, "When is it time to give up praying for certain requests that have yet to be answered? Or should I never give up praying for people, things or events that I have put before God that He had not answered?"

Someone said that God answers prayers in three ways: 1) Yes, 2) No, or 3) *Wait*, which means "the time is not right."

"Yes!" Answers

God answers many prayers with a "yes," granting requests and resolving issues. When He answers a prayer you put before

Him, the right response is to prayerfully thank Him for what He has done for you. One example of answered prayer in the Bible took place when Paul and Silas had been imprisoned because of preaching the gospel. The church prayed corporately for their release, and an angel came to open the gates of the jail and release them. What a miracle! The prompt answer to the prisoners' prayer was "Yes." From that example, God teaches us that He can answer our prayers quickly.

"No!" Answers

Sometimes when we pray for certain things, God says "No." He answers "no" due to reasons I do not know, but I do know that the Heavenly Father wishes well upon His children. He will answer "no" to some prayers because He has a better plan for the one asking. Even when His answer is difficult to accept, we must not forget that He sees all of the episodes of our life, and usually, when He doesn't open a door or when He closes a door, He plans to lead us to a blessed gate.

One "no" from God came in the apostle Paul's life. Paul probably had a medical issue involving his eyes, and when he taught publicly, his presence might have caused some uneasiness among the listeners. He prayed to God to fix his "thorn," and received the following answer:

> *"My grace is sufficient for you, for my power is made perfect in weakness." Therefore I will boast all the more gladly about my weaknesses, so that Christ's power may rest on me.*[9]

"Wait!"

When God is plainly not answering our request, He is asking us to wait. Don't force open a door that He closed or through which He does not want you to go because He better knows what He has prepared for you.

"Your eyes saw my unformed body; all the days ordained for me were written in your book before one of them came to be. How precious to me are your thoughts, God! How vast is the sum of them!"[10]

Sometimes when you pray for a specific request, He will answer, "Keep waiting," meaning the time is not yet right for the prayers to be granted. Those times of expectancy feel somewhat like sitting patiently in a waiting room for an appointment. While we await His answer, we need to continue praying, staying vigilant, and waiting for God to fulfill our request at the right time.

Genesis 25 says that Isaac began to pray for a child at 40 years of age because Rebekah was barren, and the answer to his prayer came after waiting 20 years. Isaac was 60 years old when his twin sons, Esau and Jacob, were born.[11]

Likewise, the answer to some of your prayer will come after many years, but you will have to continue praying and stay vigilant until it is fulfilled. Don't give up!

God answers prayers in three ways:
yes, no, and keep waiting.

Beyond Expectations

Elizabeth's tears, the absence of a child, and the social pressure often broke Zechariah's heart as he went toward the Temple to perform his work as a priest. A battle raged in his soul between the priest's dedicated service to God, and His stone-cold silence to Zechariah's prayers directed to Him for decades.

"Why haven't You solved my wife Elizabeth's problem of barrenness the way You did for Hannah? She was infertile, but You healed her, and she gave birth to Samuel. Sarah, who was older still, received a promise from the angels that she would give birth to a son in a year. We are faithful too, and we have prayed ardently our whole lives. God, why has our problem not been resolved?"

Many believers who have lived lives of faith embrace battles within their soul before God and His apparent indifference toward resolving certain prayer requests. I think if many people looked deep within themselves, they would see how the suffering and the failure to understand the silence of the heaven erodes their soul. Seeing the heartache and the tears caused by not understanding the divine plan flowing from the holes made by the pain would yield a turning point. Some would let the weeds of sorrow grow in the garden of their hearts that would invade their lives, while others would continue to believe that God knows better what He is doing and will continue to press the pedal of faithfulness.

Some let the weeds of sorrow grow in the garden of their hearts and invade their lives, while others continue to believe that God knows better what He is doing and will continue to press the pedal of faithfulness.

At the same time Zechariah and Elizabeth were petitioning heaven's gates for a child, the Roman yoke was pressing down on the Jews, and the corruption at the Temple was further increasing the hope that the promised Messiah would come to free the country. For 400 years, no divine revelation had taken place in the country. Heaven was quiet to this waiting nation. But at the moment when the priest Zechariah entered into the temple to perform the Holy Place service, something miraculous took place. An angel appeared to him. That appearance was a special moment for him and a historic one for a nation that had not received any divine signs for hundreds of years.

But the angel said to him: "Do not be afraid, Zechariah; your prayer has been heard. Your wife Elizabeth will bear you a son, and you are to call him John.

Zechariah asked the angel, "How can I be sure of this? I am an old man and my wife is well along in years."

The angel said to him, "I am Gabriel. I stand in the presence of God, and I have been sent to speak to you and to tell you this good news. And now you will be silent and not able to speak until the day this happens, because you did not believe my words, which will come true at their appointed time."[12]

Even if the angel's message had been one full of hope that their prayers for a son throughout the years had been heard, Zechariah still looked at the signs of aging, the biological impossibility, and doubted his message, asking for an explanation. *"How can I be sure of this? I am an old man and my wife is well along in years."[13]*

The angel quickly detected the marks of a lack of faith in the priest's question. Zechariah did not believe the angel's message because the reality of the circumstances was more palpable and stronger than the angel's promise. The impossibility due to age alone spoke to the priest louder than the angel's message.

Oftentimes in our lives, our circumstances bring worry and concern, which takes more control of us than God's promises. Like Peter, we take too long looking at the rising waves more so than at Jesus who was walking on the water right in front of us. When you look at problems and worries too much, you amplify them in your mind, and the Almighty God becomes small and powerless. The solution is to look at Him more—at His greatness and His endless power—and let His splendor and glory amaze you.

Develop an image of Him in your mind the way He is. The priest Isaiah was surrounded by problems and doubt. All he saw on the horizon was sorrow, but when he entered the Temple and had a vision that God was above the universe, his problems began to seem small.

> *"I saw the Lord, high and exalted, seated on a throne; and the train of his robe filled the temple. Above him were seraphim, each with six wings: With two wings they covered their faces, with two they covered their feet, and with two they were flying. And they were calling to one another: "Holy, holy, holy is the LORD Almighty; the whole earth is full of his glory."*[14]

We can become so accustomed to pain and sorrow that we think it is normal. Then, when we hear God's promises of a free, blessed and fulfilled life, we are unmoved and believe the message is for those who are naïve and do not know about life. But the spiritual life is full of abundance, joy and fulfillment. The fact that you are not experiencing this abundant life does not mean it does not exist.

Sometimes we are like Zechariah, asking God for logical explanations as to how He would take care of us or details as to how a specific situation would be resolved. However, if we always get logical explanations, then the element of faith will be removed from the equation.

> *"Now faith is confidence in what we hope for and assurance about what we do not see"* (Hebrews 11:1 NIV).

Faith is exercised when you pray and wait for His promises to be fulfilled—even if they haven't taken place in the material world. You keep faith that they will materialize.

"This is the confidence we have in approaching God: that if we ask anything according to his will, he hears us. And if we know that he hears us—whatever we ask—we know that we have what we asked of him" (1 John 5:14-15 NIV).

Like Peter, we look too long at the rising waves instead of at Jesus who was walking on the water.

The Factory of Faith

The angel said to him, "I am Gabriel. I stand in the presence of God, and I have been sent to speak to you and to tell you this good news. And now you will be silent and not able to speak until the day this happens, because you did not believe my words, which will come true at their appointed time."[15]

When the angel saw that the priest doubted the message, he told him that he would be mute until what was foretold would be fulfilled. In the following days, Zechariah went home and had to write everything that had happened to him for

Elizabeth. He tried to speak multiple times, but he could not pronounce words. Zechariah's new problem—muteness—was meant to permanently remind him of the promise made to him and not to speak against God's divine plan due to a lack of faith. The priest so wanted to say something, but he couldn't. His thoughts automatically went to the angel's message and the boy who would be born. Being mute told him every day that what had occurred at the Holy Place was not an illusion caused by the smoke of incense, but a reality. Being mute was the engine developing faith in him, reminding him of the birth of a boy despite the biological impossibility.

I can imagine the day when the elderly Elizabeth went to him and said, "Zechariah, I have unbelievable news; I am with child!"

Not all of our problems are meant to cause us sorrow. Just as the issue of being mute was meant to remind him of the angel's promises, some problems we have or will have are meant to develop our faith. Indeed, some problems are uncomfortable and painful, but some come with a mission—to be like a factory producing faith to remind us of His specific promises for our lives and helping us wait for them.

The spiritual battle that some have to face is keeping together the painful reality that they live in the moment and the embryo of faith planted by God's promise, which must be fed in order to develop. That is the moment when things are contradictory, but faith must prevail.

In the spiritual world, spirits are portrayed as animals. When the Word is planted, God's promises in a man's life, the birds, which symbolize the Evil One's spirits, come to steal the seeds in the ground, meaning in the mind (Matthew 13:4, 19). Any *rhema* promise you receive from God must be guarded because the birds of the Evil One will come attack and steal it.

Any rhema promise you receive from God must be guarded because the birds of the Evil One will come attack and steal it.

When God Turns the Table

After this his wife Elizabeth became pregnant and for five months remained in seclusion. "The Lord has done this for me," she said. "In these days he has shown his favor and taken away my disgrace among the people."[16]

The time had come for God to turn the table in Elizabeth's favor and to remove her disgrace. God's specialty is turning situations to His children's favor. He turned the situation for Joseph, who was at the bottom and rose to the top. He turned the table for barren Hannah who became a joyful mother among her children. He turned the circumstances for David, who was cast out by King Saul and then elevated him to become the king of the nation of Israel.

God can also turn the tables for you. God is your defender. Maybe you are down now, but He can uplift you. Maybe you feel sorrow, but He can brighten your life. Maybe you are in a disastrous financial situation, but He can change it for the better. Maybe you feel useless in this world, but He can show you your value.

The Right Time

During the months when Zechariah was mute, he had time to meditate on how God had answered their prayers and had taken away Elizabeth's disgrace at the right time. God resolved the pain the couple had endured for decades beyond their expectations. However, more was involved than Zechariah could understand. The boy who would be born would be special because his role in the history of salvation would be very important. John, the unborn son, would become the human megaphone to announce the coming of the Messiah—the One expected for thousands of years. John the Baptist was sent to a family of believers who would rear him in purity because of his divine purpose.

> *"But when the fullness of time had come, God sent forth his Son, born of woman, born under the law...."*[17]

Jesus's birth took place at the right time (the kronos) preestablished by God to bring salvation to humanity, and John the Baptist's role was to announce the Savior's coming. Zechariah's and Elizabeth's son had to be born in accordance with the coming of the Messiah.

While Zechariah and Elizabeth prayed and felt sorrow, God was setting the scene for His Son's entry into the world.

The priest Zechariah began to understand that God had a right time to work and fulfill His plans that went beyond our understanding.

"For everything there is a season, and a time for every matter under heaven. He has made everything beautiful in its time. Also, he has put into man's heart, yet so that he cannot find out what God has done from the beginning to the end."[18]

God has a right time for everything in our lives. In this society of instant everything, we would like the spiritual realm to be instantaneous as well. However, when our calendars do not sync up with God's calendar, we often try to get ahead of His plans—like Abraham did with his slave Hagar and the way Moses did with freeing the people from slavery. Waiting for the right time has an important role in heaven's calendar. We will often not understand at the moment why He does not answer certain prayers or doesn't resolve a certain situation, but later on we will understand. God lines up events beyond what our physical eyes see so that in the right timing, His good plans for us might be fulfilled.

Usually, in the midst of events, we will not fully understand what is happening, and we will want everything to be concluded quickly. As time goes by and the threads of the events that took place are tied up, we can better recognize God's divine plan. Don't get ahead of God; wait for the right time.

There is a right time that God works in,
and He lines up circumstances to fulfill
His plans that go beyond our understanding.

Tying the Threads

Elizabeth kept the fact that she was expecting a baby hidden from her neighbors and those she knew. Perhaps she was embarrassed because of her age and didn't want others to know. Some commentators have speculated that she had doubts due to the uncertainty caused by the fact that her baby was not moving. She did not know if the fetus was alive or dead. She did not want to say anything to those around so that they wouldn't think that she was being irrational in her advanced age. *"Zechariah, why isn't the baby moving? I fear something must not be right; maybe I am too old and cannot carry the pregnancy to term. I am worried that he is not moving."*

On the other hand, the angel was also sent to the virgin Mary who lived at a considerable geographical distance from Elizabeth to whom she was related.

"How will this be," Mary asked the angel, "since I am a virgin?"

The angel answered, "The Holy Spirit will come on you, and the power of the Most High will overshadow you. So the holy one to be born will be called the Son of God.

Even Elizabeth your relative is going to have a child in her old age, and she who was said to be unable to conceive is in her sixth month. For no word from God will ever fail."[19]

For young Mary, the angel's message that she was expecting a baby was news that caused much consternation. Telling her fiancé Joseph that she was with child by the Holy Spirit was not acceptable. Who would have believed her?

Had Joseph terminated their engagement in private or in public, she would have been left with a stigma her entire life. If those around would have heard that she was pregnant and the father could not be identified, she could have been stoned to death or would have lived her entire life as a pariah in social disgrace. The situation was complicated for young Mary, but the angel gave her a sign to help her in fulfilling her purpose: "Elizabeth, your older relative who was barren her whole life, is also expecting a child."

"When Elizabeth heard Mary's greeting, the baby leaped in her womb, and Elizabeth was filled with the Holy Spirit." [20]

Elizabeth needed Mary. The young woman was carrying Jesus—the Resurrection and the Life. When Mary met with Elizabeth, something miraculous happened to Elizabeth. When her unborn child felt the close presence of Jesus, he began to stir in her womb. If Elizabeth had any lack of faith about her baby, the presence of Mary and Jesus eliminated any doubt she had entertained.

Each of us carry different dreams that are yet to be born. We were excited about these dreams and prayed for them for years, but currently, they are in the embryo stage. We do not know if they will see the light of day or will die in the womb of the imagination. Perhaps you have dreamed of building a ministry or a business or a house. Perhaps you desire to write a book. Perhaps you have entertained the idea of a new career. Perhaps doubts are now knocking on your mind's door, and you no longer know if the dream is still alive or dead.

People like Mary bring with them *resurrection* and *life* and make dreams start to move and kick, as John the Baptist did in his mother's womb. Those kinds of people have an outstanding charisma for resuscitating the dreams in another person's life. On the other hand, Joseph's envious brothers killed the dreams in Joseph's life and then sold him as a slave. The difference between Mary, the mother of Jesus, and Joseph's brothers is that some bring life to dreams and make them come true, and others kill dreams. Surround yourself with those who bring life.

Even if Mary and Elizabeth were not understood in their circle of friends and by those around them, they were still part of the same vision revealed by the angel. Surround yourself with people who go where you are going and who have the same vision as you do because they will understand your struggles and will give you the best wings when you are down.

*The difference between Mary and
Joseph's brothers is that some bring life to dreams
and make them come true, and others
kill dreams.*

Mary needed Elizabeth's experience. Young Mary was experiencing a period of not being understood by those around her. Facing the accusations and gossip of others would not help her understand God's plan for her. She needed someone with experience to teach her how to use a shield to guard herself from the arrows of censure that would soon be released at her. Elizabeth knew all about the accusations of others and not understanding divine plans; her lifetime of experience made her the best mentor.

The press of suffering that Elizabeth went through created a precious oil to be used to light young Mary's path through the thick forest of unknown she was facing. Now came the time for Elizabeth to understand that none of her suffering was in vain. In fact, the years of suffering represented the school where she had learned the hard lessons to be able to help the young woman who carried the Savior of the world.

In the following months, Elizabeth taught Mary how to live and to accept God's plan that seemed unintelligible, and yet in which both were involved. When something big is involved in a divine plan, don't expect accomplishing it to be easy, but you can succeed with God's help and associating with the right people.

Have you ever wondered if the suffering that you have experienced for months or even years has any purpose? Is there something greater than we can see associated with our suffering? I want to remind you that the experience and lessons you learned in the hard moments of life are the oil that will light the path of other "Marys" traversing the thick forest of the unknown and help them understand some of the divine plan. In God's plan, your suffering is not in vain and has a purpose beyond what you understand now. God wants you to use your past experiences, both painful and beautiful, to support others. Elizabeth had a role in Mary's life, and you can have a role in the lives of other Marys.

In conclusion, what I have seen from the experience of these three and from personal experience is the following:

- God works beyond our expectations and changes the situation at the right time.

- The pain or olive press has a purpose in His plan, and the oil will be used to uplift others.

- Even though you do not understand what is happening at the moment, continue to be faithful to Him and, at the right time, He will answer you.

- Surround yourself with Marys who can help resurrect your dreams.

Reflection Group Questions

1. Have you ever experienced tension between living in spiritual purity and accusations from others? If yes, explain the tension you have experienced.

2. In what way do the cultural and religious mindsets create victims? How can a person escape these cultural and religious mindsets?

3. What does the oil press of suffering mean to you? Why does God allow the press of suffering in our lives? What has been accomplished in your life by passing through the press?

4. Share an experience when the answer to your prayers has been either: "yes," "no," or "keep waiting." What did you learn through each answer? Reflect on what you learned when the answer God provided did not match what you were expecting.

5. In what way has the oil produced through the press of suffering been used in your life to uplift others?

6. Share an experience when the outcome only made sense when looking at the events in your life retrospectively. What did you learn about understanding God through this process?

CHAPTER TWO

In the Footsteps
of a Fugitive

"The church is not a museum for saints but a hospital for sinners."

– Morton Kelsey

"I appeal to you to show kindness to my child, Onesimus. I became his father in the faith while here in prison. Onesimus hasn't been of much use to you in the past, but now he is very useful to both of us. I am sending him back to you, and with him comes my own heart."

– Philemon 10-12 (NLT)

DURING THE AD 60s, the Roman Empire owned approximately 60 million slaves. The philosopher Aristotle said, "The slave is a living tool, a speaking tool."[21] These so-called "speaking instruments" with no rights, whose masters had full rights over their life and death, still had dreams, emotions, and inner workings; in other words, they were living souls.

Of those 60 million speaking instruments living at that time in the Roman Empire, the Bible places its lens on a young slave named Onesimus and describes his life and experiences. He was a slave on the wealthy Philemon's estate, but he loathed the orders that he promptly had to fulfill and the daily work he had to perform. He had often heard other slaves' stories about the big city of Rome with its impressive circuses, free bread, and the colorful multitudes of free people and slaves who walked the streets of the city. In his soul as he began to harbor the illusion of a free life in the big city, he let his thoughts fly free. He started to dream of another life—an independent life that he could live as he wanted, without so many boundaries.

If I could only get to Rome, no one will tell me what to do any longer. I can go where I want and stay as long as I want. I am still young; I can start a new life. According to the older slaves, Rome is the city of possibilities. If I manage to run away from my master, no one will find me in that crowd. But what if he does find me? What if he does catch me? I know that the slaves who run away from their masters often receive harsh punishment or are even put to death. Is running away worth it? I don't think anyone will catch me. I am young, and I will run away to freedom and happiness as far as my legs will take me.

Emboldened by the illusion of freedom and a life without impositions, he began dreaming of Rome every day. Young Onesimus was in the pursuit of freedom and happiness and was ready to risk everything to get to it. After preparing his small bag with food ahead of time, one day he stole money from Philemon's home and ran away toward the city that promised his ideal. He secretly crossed the 1,200 miles between the cities of Colossae and Rome as fast as he could, heading to the city of all possibilities.

Having reached Rome, the most fascinating metropolis of the time, he was impressed by the imposing buildings, the dynamic life to which he was unaccustomed, and the myriad of people. Not knowing the social life and system in Rome, the money he had was quickly spent. Hungry, with no money, he stole some food and was subsequently caught and thrown in jail.

For young Onesimus, the illusion of a happy, free, and boundless life quickly fell apart in the city that had held the promise of the ideal. A slave from the province found balancing the world of Rome, so free and full of traps, was difficult. Thus, the reality of life hit him abruptly; he had been pursuing happiness, but he ended up chained in prison.

In these days, how many people pursue happiness and a life they can live without boundaries? People all around us are fueled by all types of illusions that have conquered their hearts or according to various unheard-of promises race in pursuit of lasting happiness. But the quicker the choice, the faster the promises seem to fade into the horizon, moving to the next hill. *If I could just get there, or if I could just accomplish that goal or finish that contract, certainly I will be fulfilled.* But in the race to the promised happiness only "a little bit farther," we realize that we've run a long way without accomplishing any result, or even that we've run in the wrong direction. When we wake up from running, we realize that we have been caught in different traps or invisible prisons of the soul where we find ourselves chained up for a long time and where others stay forever.

The young prisoner Onesimus found himself bound by the cuffs of regret. In the cold Roman prison cell, his negative thoughts began to circle like vultures ready to devour his peace and quiet for a long time.

You are young, but your future looks bleak. Staying and working for Philemon would have been far better than this. There you had fresh meals and could gather around the fire with your peers and laugh and talk together. You were an idiot to let yourself be guided by illusions. Look where you ended up. What will become of your life now?

Many people who allow the winds of illusions and false promises to push the sails of their ship end up imprisoned by different spiritual, financial, social, or relational issues. They later wake up from the illusory race full of regret, remorseful in their minds and souls about the decisions of the past and overly worried about the dismal future opening up before them. There is no taming the voice of regret echoing in the chamber of their minds.

The prison of regret, remorse and worry is the most fertile ground for the seeds of doubt of God's plan and benevolence. When joy appears briefly, Satan sneaks in through the mind's backdoor to remind us of the list of sins we have committed; he uses our past mistakes and failures to sabotage our potential and the future that lies before us. The handcuffs that the Devil places on the soul revolve around the doubt that something better might lie ahead. He makes you consume energy with regrets of what you have done and the whisper that no one around will understand you or accept you.

> *"For the accuser of our brothers and sisters has been thrown down to earth—the one who accuses them before our God day and night"* (Revelation 12:10 NLT).

When you become mired in difficult situations because of mistakes or traps set by the Evil One, those around you will often make you feel like a failure—like a wrecked ship with punctures too big to be mended. They specialize in merciless labeling and anchoring your life's wrecked ship in the muddy waters of the dirty past. They want to keep you a prisoner of your failed experiences at all costs. If you haven't experienced this quagmire yourself, you certainly have seen this taking place in the lives of others.

The good news is that God wants to heal those who face such conditions and whose lives have been shattered. God specializes in restoring shattered lives and making something beautiful out of them. When those around us scrutinize us with judgmental eyes and categorize us as failures, God looks at us with the eyes of a jeweler who sees the value of the diamond beyond the rough, tinted surface. God specializes in restoring and creating impressive stained glass out of the failures of our lives. He is a specialist at making trophies of the weak for His glory.

> *"For we do not have a high priest who is unable to empathize with our weaknesses, but we have one who has been tempted in every way, just as we are—yet he did not sin"*
> (Hebrews 4:15 NIV).

For this very reason Jesus came into the world—for the sinful, for the failed. God accepts us and receives as us as we are: wrecked ships.

> *Later, Matthew invited Jesus and his disciples to his home as dinner guests, along with many tax collectors and other disreputable sinners. But when the Pharisees saw this, they asked his disciples, "Why does your teacher eat with such scum?" When Jesus heard this, he said, "Healthy people don't need a doctor—sick people do." Then he added, "Now go and learn the meaning of this Scripture: 'I want you to show mercy, not offer sacrifices.' For I have come to call not those who think they are righteous, but those who know they are sinners"*
> (Matthew 9:10-13 NLT).

Grace tells us that we are accepted just as we are. We may not be the kind of people we want to be, we may be a long way from our goals, we may have more failures than achievements, we may not be wealthy or powerful or spiritual, we may not even be happy, but we are nonetheless accepted by God, held in his hands. Such is his promise to us in Jesus Christ, a promise we can trust.[22]

God likes to work with the shards that are completely handed over to Him; He likes to create stained-glass masterpieces from the failures of our lives.

Illusions in the Pursuit of Happiness

If we do not confront the illusions that settle into our minds and souls and instead allow them to guide us, they often lead us into directions where we realize we never intended to head. Sometimes we don't want to hear the truth because we do not want the illusions that we harbored and developed in our minds to be destroyed.

Barbara Grizzuti Harrison said, "Belief in the absence of illusions is itself an illusion."[23] Therefore, we need to constantly set the illusions of different promises and ideals side by side with the Word of God. I have seen certain illusions knocking on many people's doors that must be confronted.

The Illusion that Actions Do Not Have Consequences

This illusion promises that you can live in any way you please and the bill will never come. You can consume as much as you want because the waiter will never come to bring you the bill. Many people only understand the consequences of their unwise decisions when the knock sounds on their life's door, and the bill is presented. Onesimus believed more in the speed of his legs and that no one would catch him than he did in the fact that decisions had consequences.

When Absalom made some dire mistakes, his father, King David, did not punish him, but was quite lenient with him. Had someone else in the kingdom made the same mistakes, that person would have been punished grievously and immediately. When you make mistakes in life and consequences are not forthcoming, you start to allow yourself even bigger mistakes. *They forgave me once, they will forgive me again; I am certain of it* becomes the pervading thought.

Young Prince Absalom attracted many followers and then organized a coup to proclaim himself king. When David heard that his son was staging a revolution, he ran away with the people closest to him and set up a small army in the desert. In his madness, the power-hungry Absalom began to fight his father. David told the people, *"If you fight with Absalom, take care of him. "For my sake, deal gently with young Absalom."*[24] In other words, David was saying, "Don't do any harm to this unruly prince."

Absalom thought that no matter what happened, the king would forgive him, and his actions would bring no drastic consequences. However, General Joab, a warrior whose sword had been bloodied all throughout his life, thought differently. In the midst of battle, when Absalom retreated on his mule into a thick forest, his long, windblown hair caught in a tree's branches and dragged him from his mount. The prince could not free himself from the clutching branches. Joab saw him hanging defenseless. As the general considered the trouble this king's son had brought on the nation—the death of many innocent people, the usurping of power, the breaking of his father's heart, Joab realized that he had to be punished for his years of wrongdoing. Joab brought judgment to Absalom when he shot three arrows into his heart, thus ending the life of the prince who wrongly thought that actions did not have consequences.

Likewise, many people still have this illusion that their

actions, either done in hiding or in public view, do not come with any consequences. Many erroneously think that they can hide their deeds, whether good or bad, and since no one will know about them, they cannot be touched. Perhaps the person is held in high repute on the social ladder. However, the law that God set up for the universe says that sooner or later, every action will bring consequences. "You will always harvest what you plant."[25]

What you do when you are twenty years old will have consequences at thirty. Every action is like a seed planted in the ground that will eventually bear fruit; its effects will show. Thinking that what you do carries no repercussions is a false illusion.

> "For he who does wrong will receive the consequences of the wrong which he has done, and that without partiality" (Colossians 3:25 NASB).

> "For the time is coming when everything that is covered will be revealed, and all that is secret will be made known to all" (Matthew 10:26b NLT).

The Illusion of False Promises

False promises are sweet and bring the illusion of a sweet taste that will remain permanently, but we must not forget that bogus assurances bring sorrow. We often allow ourselves to be driven by appearances or false promises in the same way that Onesimus allowed himself to be fooled. He thought that real life and a slice of heaven could be found in Rome. However, beyond the appearances and the brilliance, many tragedies and much pain could be found on the streets of Rome.

I remember reading about the hero Ulysses passing by the Island of the Sirens with his ship and crew. Mermaids are described in Greek mythology as being half woman, half bird. Their songs enticed the sailors passing by the island with promises that they could enjoy unheard-of pleasures. The sailors, who could not resist the sirens' songs of promise, steered their ships toward their island, striking the rocks hidden by the surf. As their ships were ripped apart in those choppy waters, the sailors lost their lives.

When Ulysses approached the Island of the Sirens, he wanted to hear the song without losing his life. He poured wax into his sailors' ears so that they would not hear the sirens' tempting song. He had his men bind him to the mast so that he alone could hear the song but would be unable to steer his ship in that direction. Tempted by their song, Ulysses struggled to free himself and begged his men to free him. However, his plan worked and saved him from the sirens' song; he could not free himself from the ropes, and the sailors could not hear his pleas. He alone heard the enchanting song of the sirens and survived.

Many of today's Ulysses have steered the ship of their lives straight toward various sirens promising joy and delights they had never before experienced. Many modern-day Ulysses have ended up shipwrecked perhaps in multiple aspects of their lives. Some have wrecked their careers, others their families, and others their health. Many attractions that seem so promising will often be a trap with jagged rocks hidden behind them.

The grass will always be greener and more appealing in the neighbor's yard on the other side of the fence. Just as Ulysses used ropes to restrain himself and avoid death, setting strict and well-defined boundaries in our lives will keep us from many failures if we will respect them.

> *"So don't be misled, my dear brothers and sisters. Whatever is good and perfect is a gift coming down to us from God our Father, who created all the lights in the heavens. He never changes or casts a shifting shadow."*[26]

The Word of God tells that any good and perfect gift comes from God, but Satan promises and wants to deceive through his poisonous gifts. If we look more closely at Satan's strategy, we can see the bag full of promises, lies and the illusion that the gifts he brings before you are perfect. He promises that under his protection you will be able to taste everything he brings because you are armored, and no one will see you. Furthermore, he offers a unique opportunity that you must take advantage of now, and no one will know what you have done.

That cart full of poisonous apples that Satan brings you appears to be good and promising, but once you take a bite, he appears from behind the curtain that he promised was armored and starts to embarrass you in front of everyone. Like a drummer, he starts to play the beat, announcing your mistakes and sins to everyone. He specializes in bringing shame and remorse into people's lives.

Pray and ask God to help you so that you may differentiate between the gifts that come to you from Him and those that are illusions—the Evil One's inviting traps.

The Illusion of Material Possessions

We all likely remember the story of the young boy and the golden windows. Every evening after helping his father with the day's work, his father would give him an hour to play. The boy would climb to the top of the hill and look into the distance at the next hill and see gleaming windows made of gold in a house on the far-off hill. How he desired to go to that place. One day, he walked to the neighboring hill to see the house with the golden windows. To his surprise and sadness, he saw that that the house had normal glass windows.

When a little girl came out to enquire why he was there, he asked, "Where is the house with golden windows that I see here every day?"

The little girl replied, "You are in the wrong place!" She pointed to another house that she could see with golden windows at dusk. "There is the house with the golden windows!"

To his utter surprise, he realized he was looking at his own house![27]

So many people run to reach the house with golden windows. Unfortunately, the house can never be reached and only moves farther and farther away from one hill to another. The faster the person runs, the faster the unreachable goal seems to move into the distance. Some chase after it, thinking that material possessions or a higher standard of living will fulfill the deepest needs of their soul, but this chase only ensnares them in a vicious circle. Some only awaken from this cycle at the end of their lives, and sadly, others never do.

Some people in this world who have nothing or noticeably little have decided to be happy. On the other hand, others who have much are unhappy. Happiness promised by material possessions is an illusion that will keep many trapped in a race, chasing after a mirage in the desert of this world.

> *"Do not toil to acquire wealth; be discerning enough to desist. When your eyes light on it, it is gone, for suddenly it sprouts wings, flying like an eagle toward heaven"*
> (Proverbs 23:4-5 ESV).

> *"Blessed is the one who finds wisdom, and the one who gets understanding, for the gain from her is better than gain from silver and her profit better than gold. She is more precious than jewels, and nothing you desire can compare with her. Long life is in her right hand; in her left hand are riches and honor"* (Proverbs 3:13-16).

The Illusion in the Mind

Many fall into yet another trap—that of the ideas that they create, believe, and nurture without allowing anyone else to advise them. The wise man who wants to be successful will surround himself with people who will examine his illusions or ideas with truth and experience.

I remember a man I will call John, who had a beautiful family, an outstanding wife and three children. John was driven by the idea of owning his own newspaper business. He fostered the idea in his mind and didn't tell anyone about it because he was afraid that someone would steal his business idea. One day, he sold his house and invested all of his money into that venture, without considering other obstacles or unforeseen factors.

The newspaper did not sell the way he had imagined. The companies he had hoped would place advertisements in his newspaper did not contact him and investors never showed up. He quickly ran out of money, went bankrupt and ended up without a house in which to live.

Beginning from its infancy, his idea or illusion should have been studied and carefully researched. Had John conducted market research, he would have known whether or not he had an opportunity to turn his idea into a successful business. Before selling his house and sinking his money into a newspaper, he should have written a business plan, chosen a location, planned the structure of the business, and looked at funding his venture. Seeking the advice and experience of others would have been helpful and adhering to biblical principles would have been met with more success.

We often foster different ideas in our minds or have certain illusions we hold tightly, and we don't want to tell others because they might confront us and tell us the truth, destroying and ruining our imaginary ideal where we like to take refuge. However, allowing the lens of the Bible or close friends to confront our ideas are far better than facing bankruptcy as in John's case.

"So don't go to war without wise guidance; victory depends on having many advisers" (Proverbs 24:6 NLT).

"Plans go wrong for lack of advice; many advisers bring success" (Proverbs 15:22 NLT).

Ask God to help you to differentiate between the gifts that come to you from Him and those who are the Evil One's hook.

The Crossroad

Sometimes, prisoners are curious to hear about the circumstances or events that brought others behind bars. Prison becomes a mini-society where friendships and rivalries develop as well as a place where God can reach and work beyond the closed doors of regrets and remorse that haunt its confines.

I wonder how many people live their lives locked up in the closed cells of regret because of unwise decisions they have made and are so haunted by remorse that they allow no one in and refuse to open the door to freedom. The loneliness haunted by regret and remorse is the room where God permeates and gives them an audience.

Paul of old was also a part of that small society of prisoners, but he had not been imprisoned due to theft or other crimes, but because of preaching the gospel. The apostle treated every place and every person as a part of his boundless parish. He was a man fulfilling his calling as he preached the gospel—even in the most difficult of places.

When the imprisoned Onesimus crossed paths with Paul, the apostle asked, "What's your name, young man?"

"I am Onesimus."

"Oh, yours is a beautiful name meaning *useful*. May the good Lord help you be useful in His kingdom. How did you end up in this place?"

"I was hungry, so I stole some bread, and I was caught," the young man snapped curtly.

"Where are you from, Onesimus?"

"I am from far away, near Colossae."

"I have a good friend near Colossae, a brother in the faith whose name is Philemon. Perhaps you might know him."

"Philemon? My former master from where I left—his name is Philemon. Umm…from where I fled…."

Even if Onesimus had left that statement hanging without sharing too many details, Paul realized the prisoner's truthful last words meant that he had taken his life into his own hands. He had driven the car of his life on the most dangerous of race-tracks and had crashed it. In that time everyone knew that a slave's flight from his master meant death, and the image that Paul read on that young man's face was a death sentence.

At that crossroad between the fugitive Onesimus and the apostle Paul, God was, in fact, orchestrating a divine appointment. Oftentimes, in the discouraging events or failures we experience, He brings different people across our path to bring us a message. These messengers are like a switch that can change our lives.

> A divine appointment is a meeting with another person that has been specifically and unmistakably ordered by God.[28]

These meetings are supernaturally scheduled and organized so that His plans may develop in our lives. Sometimes we miss these meetings scheduled by Him because we are too busy with our agenda, and our spiritual radar is turned off. Often things, people or events that appear in our paths and do not correspond to our plans are politely pushed aside or ignored. We are apt to forget that God uses this method and brings these meetings for a purpose. Of course, if God orchestrates divine appointments, the Evil One also arranges his own malevolent appointments.

At other times, when our future plans change almost overnight, we are redirected from our outlined path to a detour that we do not understand. When we experience delays in what we have decided to do, we start to categorize these experiences or moments as failures, forgetting they are God's way to intervene in our agendas and to redirect us to His plans. He often uses inconveniences in our lives for a precise purpose, and we must remember to look at them through the lens of a divine appointment.

Divine appointments supernaturally scheduled and organized so that His plans may develop in our lives.

I have noticed that we only accept certain messages, redirections and changes in action or character traits after we experience certain failures, impossibilities, or "prisons" in which we are caught.

When Onesimus was caught between a rock and a hard place—his future in prison and punishment for being a fugitive slave, he opened his ear to listen to Paul. *Perhaps there is a solution even for the shards of my life.* When life puts us under the doctor's scalpel, and he tells us that the surgery might not succeed and that life is short, a new world opens up before us. Though the divine had not formerly interested us, then we easily put aside the illusions and ambitions we had and pray, asking God to guide the doctor's scalpel. Those are divine appointments—moments when He invites us to redirect our gaze upward. These are moments when the Great Engineer, God, orchestrates unexpected meetings and creates different circumstances to reconnect us with Him.

Divine appointments are not only orchestrated through negative-appearing circumstances, but also through blessings beyond measure that come into our lives. When the disciples had struggled all night fishing and didn't catch anything, Jesus told them, "Throw out your net on the right-hand side of the boat, and you'll get some!"[29]

Upon His command, a school of fish started to swim into the disciples' nets, and a failed night of fishing turned into a morning of success. The disciples' cache of fish was so great, they couldn't even draw in the net. After this experience, one of the disciples suddenly saw something more in their success. He understood that the hand of God gave them the idea and had blessed them.

> Then the disciple Jesus loved said to Peter, "It's the Lord!" When Simon Peter heard that it was the Lord, he put on his tunic (for he had stripped for work), jumped into the water, and headed to shore.[30]

The great blessings that come into your life are planned by Him as divine appointments with specific purposes. Sometimes God uses this method of "divine appointments" to redirect us, to help us accept a message, to help us let go of certain things, and to bring us a new perspective. Of course, His purposes and plans are often beyond our capability to understand.

By the way, in this situation, the disciples were miraculously blessed so that they could look back to Jesus and return to the work that they had abandoned that still needed to be completed.

At other times, He uses us as instruments to help those around us to connect to God the way Paul was used in the life of Onesimus.

"So when the Midianite merchants came by, his brothers pulled Joseph up out of the cistern and sold him for twenty shekels of silver to the Ishmaelites, who took him to Egypt."[31]

In his book, *Joseph and His Brothers,* Thomas Mann shares a conversation a Midianite may have had with young Joseph.

"Where are you taking me?" Joseph asked Kedema, one of the old man's sons....

Kedema looked him up and down. "The truth is that we are not taking you anywhere. You are with us by chance because my father bought you from the harsh masters, and you go with us wherever we will go. But this cannot be called 'taking you.'"

"No? Perhaps not," Joseph replied. "I just wanted to know this much: where is God leading me, while I go with you?"

"You are a silly young man," the Midianite answered him.... "You figure that we travel so that you can reach a specific place, where your God wants you to go."

"I hadn't thought of something like that," Joseph replied. "I know that you, my masters, travel following your own goals or as you see fit, and I did not mean to insult your dignity or your independence with my questions. But, you see, the world has many centers, one for each being and other different circles lie around it. You are only at elbow's length from me, but a universal circle surrounds you, of which you are the center, and not me. And I am the center of my circle. Both of our circles are not far from each other, not only do they touch, but God so deeply intertwined them that you, the Ishmaelites, of course, travel with all the freedom and to your heart's content, while also in the place where the two circles intertwine, there is in the middle the tool that will allow me to reach my own objective. This is why I asked where you were leading me."

"I will tell the old man, my father, how you dare to act like a wise guy, to meddle into such knowledge, to claim that you have a circle in the world especially for you and that our purpose is to be your guides.... Don't you worry, I'll tell him!"[32]

I like the way that Thomas Mann highlights Joseph's meeting with the Midianites as being a divine appointment orchestrated by God. We must attain the maturity level to accept and believe that God uses even the Midianites, who seem to be stealing our bright future and our best, to fulfill some grander plans that we will understand years later. Could you accept that an illness, a disability, a lack, a loss, a betrayal, or a failure can be an instrument in God's hands to uplift you and bless others?

Joseph told his brothers whom he met years and years later when he was a vice-pharaoh, the second most powerful man in the world: *"As for you, you meant evil against me, but God meant it for good, to bring it about that many people should be kept alive, as they are today."*[33]

"And we know that in all things God works for the good of those who love him, who have been called according to his purpose."[34]

Could you accept that an illness, a disability, a lack, a loss, a betrayal, or a failure could be an instrument in God's hand to uplift you and bless others?

Salvation

When a person finds himself in life's most horrible circumstances, could God really still turn the bad into good? Certainly, yes. God can turn any disastrous situation in your life to your favor while still preparing you for His plans!

For Onesimus, getting out of jail may have meant punishment as a fugitive slave, and jail meant punishment for theft. He was caught between a rock and a hard place, but God turned the bad into a greater good. He worked to redirect Onesimus toward His plans.

The apostle Paul realized that the young man needed forgiveness, the accusations against him removed, and the freedom that comes from God, which surpasses the present circumstances. Onesimus needed spiritual freedom of the soul and spirit that went beyond what was seen or felt.

"Young man," the apostle Paul said, "See the *cheirographon* at the door of the cell where you are? That handwritten parchment contains a list of all of the mistakes you have made, all the accusations against you, and the punishment you must endure for them. If you get rid of them, you will be free."

"Is that so?" Onesimus asked.

"Let me tell you about another prison—a spiritual one in which your soul is a prisoner. At the door of that prison a *cheirographon* lists all of the sins you have committed in this world and all of the charges against you. Those charges and accusations are before God and can be eternal. If you get rid of that *cheirographon* from the door of your spiritual jail, you will live in a spiritual freedom like you have never before experienced; you will have a new life—even in prison. The freedom and joy that God brings to your soul when your sins are forgiven, and you are transferred from the kingdom of darkness into His kingdom goes beyond the conditions you are now experiencing. Do you want to know how you can achieve forgiveness and salvation from the mistakes and accusations listed on the *cheirographon*?"

"Yes!" Onesimus listened with curiosity.

"On Golgotha, Jesus Christ was crucified on the cross for each of our sins. 'He himself bore our sins' in his body on the cross, so that we might die to sins and live for righteousness; 'by his wounds you have been healed.'[35]

"He took the *cheirographon* parchment where our sins were written and nailed it to the cross. In the moment of His crucifixion, His blood flowed over the parchment and cleansed it. *'He canceled the record* [cheirographon] *of the charges against us and took it away by nailing it to the cross.'*"[36]

The apostle Paul explained what salvation meant and there

in the Roman jail, Onesimus accepted Jesus as his Lord and Savior to bring him freedom from sins and spiritual freedom. He became Paul's spiritual child, who taught him how to live in the freedom and joy of God beyond his present conditions.

In Onesimus, we recognize the image of the human race led by the whip of instincts in the pursuit of happiness and freedom while sinking deeper in the mud of mistakes and sins. Just like God saw value in Onesimus, He also sees value in us and creates divine appointments to make us meet His divine grace. Christ brought salvation for every man, and this salvation can be received through faith. Salvation is God's gift for each of us. *"For our sake he made the sinless one a victim for sin, so that in him we might become the uprightness of God."*[37]

I like the way that Brennan Manning describes Jesus's encounter with our failures in his book titled *The Ragamuffin Gospel:*

> Jesus has journeyed to the far reaches of loneliness. In His broken body He has carried your sins and mine, every separation and loss, every heart broken, every wound of the spirit that refuses to close, all the riven experiences of men, women, and children across the bands of time.[38]

Fyodor Dostoyevsky highlighted the very fact that Christ came for the failed sinners, and not for the immaculate.

> At the last Judgment Christ will say to us, "Come, you also! Come, drunkards! Come, weaklings! Come, children of shame!"

And he will say to us: "Vile beings, you who are in the image of the beast and bear his mark, but come all the same, you as well."

And the wise and the prudent will say, "Lord, why do you welcome them?" And he will say: "If I welcome them, you wise men, if I welcome them, you prudent men, it is because not one of them has ever been judged worthy."

And he will stretch out his arms, and we will fall at his feet, and we will cry out sobbing, and then we will understand all, we will understand the Gospel of grace! Lord, your Kingdom come![39]

Another important aspect to consider is each person who is forgiven for his sins will experience moments of remorse brought on by the Evil One. Satan often rips the *chierographon* parchment with our sins from Christ's cross and waves it in front of our eyes, reminding us of the mistakes of the past. His efforts are always meant to tie us to our sinful past or to the wounds we have and pull us down from our path. When the Evil One reminds you of your past, remind him of his future.

When he will remind you of the sins and mistakes of the past, proclaim the forgiveness that you have received and thank God for that forgiveness. Sometimes you will need to loudly proclaim your thankfulness. Quote 1 John 1:9 as you proclaim His forgiveness: *"If we confess our sins, he is faithful and just to forgive us our sins, and to cleanse us from all unrighteousness."*

If we confess our sins, he is faithful and just to forgive us our sins, and to cleanse us from all unrighteousness.[40]

The Mediator

When the time came for Onesimus to be released from jail, Paul wrote a letter to his personal friend Philemon. On behalf of the runaway slave, Paul explained that young Onesimus had become a brother-in-Christ. The apostle mediated the conflict between Onesimus and the wealthy Philemon and was ready to pay from his own pocket any damage that the young man had caused.

> *"So if you consider me your partner, welcome him as you would welcome me. If he has wronged you in any way or owes you anything, charge it to me. I, PAUL, WRITE THIS WITH MY OWN HAND: I WILL REPAY IT. AND I WON'T MENTION THAT YOU OWE ME YOUR VERY SOUL! Yes, my brother, please do me this favor for the Lord's sake. Give me this encouragement in Christ."*[41]

Paul took on the role of a mediator between the two. A *mediator* is a person who has credibility before the two conflicting parties and arbitrates to mend a broken relationship. The apostle, of course, learned this role from Jesus Christ:

"For there is one God, and there is one mediator between God and men, the man Christ Jesus."[42]

The Bible contains record of other mediators: Moses mediated between the people and God, Abraham mediated for Sodom and Gomorrah so that they would not be destroyed, and Job stood up for the orphan and the widow and mediated for them.

In this society of speed, fulfillment of personal agenda and broken relationships, the great need is for mediators to come out of their personal comfort zone and help those who have made mistakes, wrecked their ships and need help to mend their lives.

The apostle Paul's letter of mediation and as a man ready to pay for Onesimus's mistakes and damage offers us a model to do the same for the Onesimuses that cross our paths in life. Sometimes we might be called to mediate in simple ways for those around us, but other times our compassion for others will call us to mediate at a deeper and more difficult level like Christ who mediated for people fallen into sin. Be a mediator for the one who is defeated; also serve as a mediator for those who are in broken relationships. *Imitatio Christi!*

For there is one God, and there is one mediator between God and men, the man Christ Jesus.[43]

Tests

Repairing the Past

Having been released from jail with Paul's letter in his hand, Onesimus was facing another test: succumb to the appealing glimmer of Rome's calling him to try again now that he possessed more knowledge, or to return to Philemon with Paul's letter mediating for him and with salvation in his soul. For Onesimus, returning to Philemon was a hard test, even with the letter in his hand because he did not know if the master would forgive him or punish him severely or even kill him.

What would you have done if you were in his place? Would you have chosen Rome or Philemon? Repairing the mistakes of the past is an extremely difficult test for each of us. Many prefer to leave the past untouched, somewhat swept under the rug of time, rather than dig through old wounds or mistakes of the past.

When Jesus entered Zacchaeus's house, the head of the tax collectors, who made his wealth through theft of taxes, he received salvation of the soul. At the table with the Savior and the disciples, he made a promise about the mistakes and sins of the past: *"if I have cheated anybody out of anything, I will pay back four times the amount."*[44]

For Zacchaeus, salvation came with making right what he had done wrong. Attempting to fix the mistakes of the past is a difficult business because opening the wounds of the past often reveals painful, noxious, rotting flesh. Unfortunately, unhealed wounds will not always be resolved; each of us, though, has a duty to repair what can be repaired.

Imagine Onesimus standing at the door of the prison, squeezing the parchment in his palms while the tension grew in the recently converted young man's soul. *Will the Christian Philemon really forgive me unconditionally as God forgave me unconditionally, or will he punish me with a whip, or will he kill me?*

Onesimus passed a difficult test as he turned his back on Rome and headed to Colossae. When he entered the doors to Philemon's estate, some slaves were happy to see him. Others' eyes widened as they pitied him, knowing what would happen. Philemon was immediately advised that the fugitive, Onesimus, had returned.

The master probably went outside right away, loudly announcing, "Prepare the whip, slave. I will teach you a lesson that's going to hurt, and from it, others will also learn. Your punishment will be akin to death."

Before Philemon signaled for the whip to be applied, the young man fell to his knees and pleaded, "Master, please forgive me for what I have done. I recognize my mistakes, and I want to tell you that I have changed." He held out Paul's letter to his master. "I have a letter for you attesting to…"

"Fugitive slave, I know how you have changed. But who do you know that would send me a letter?" Philemon asked.

"The letter was written by a prisoner I met, who says he is your friend."

Philemon snarled, "I don't have any convict friends. I am not interested in befriending thieves and fugitives."

Out of curiosity, he opened the letter and began to read.

Onesimus stood before him shaking. Two massive slaves stood with the whips in their hands, waiting for their master's command. The other slaves watched the proceedings as though they were attending a show in the Colosseum. Philemon's eyes ran through the few lines that Paul had penned to his friend:

> *"I appeal to you to show kindness to my child, Onesimus. I became his father in the faith while here in prison. Onesimus hasn't been of much use to you in the past, but now he is very useful to both of us. I am sending him back to you, and with him comes my own heart.*
>
> *I wanted to keep him here with me while I am in these chains for preaching the Good News, and he would have helped me on your behalf. But I didn't want to do anything without your consent. I wanted you to help because you were willing, not because you were forced. It seems you lost Onesimus for a little while so that you could have him back forever. He is no longer like a slave to you. He is more than a slave, for he is a beloved brother, especially to me. Now he will mean much more to you, both as a man and as a brother in the Lord.*
>
> *So if you consider me your partner, welcome him as you would welcome me. If he has wronged you in any way or owes you anything, charge it to me. I, PAUL, WRITE THIS WITH MY OWN HAND: I WILL REPAY IT. AND I WON'T MENTION THAT YOU OWE ME YOUR VERY SOUL! Yes, my brother, please do me this favor for the Lord's sake. Give me this encouragement in Christ."*[45]

After Philemon finished reading the letter written on papyrus, he lifted his tearful eyes and spoke two words to the shaking slave: "Brother Onesimus!"

Onesimus had passed the test of confessing his sins well, and Philemon had also passed the test of forgiveness.

In a life of faith, confessing your sins and offering forgiveness to others as God has granted it to you are two difficult tests that we must constantly pass. Sometimes you will have to ask for forgiveness, and other times you will have to offer it. You will constantly encounter these tests, but if you don't pass them, you will not be able to advance in a life of faith. Instead, you will have to constantly hide "on the streets of Rome," and you will ultimately sabotage God's plan for your life.

Confession of wrongs and forgiveness that you must grant to others are tests you will constantly have to pass; however, if you don't pass them, you will sabotage God's plan for your life.

The Test of Labels

Another test that both Philemon and Onesimus had to pass was *the test of labels*. Philemon had to see and consider the fugitive slave who had caused him losses as a "beloved brother." Like the apostle Paul had recommended, Philemon had to give up holding Onesimus tied to the mistakes of the past and to see him as *a beloved brother* who was important in the eyes of God and with whom he will inherit heaven.

Your past will always be a source of labels for many people who will use your mistakes to define you and create your identity based on what you have done as well as constantly reminding you of them. The apostle Paul tells Philemon and tells us as well not to keep people prisoners of past wrongs, but to remove labels and to see them as brothers in God. We need to stop ourselves, in turn, from falling into the trap of allowing ourselves to be influenced by the labels placed on us by others.

You are a beloved son; that is how God sees you. You are a beloved daughter; that is how God sees you.

Just as Paul saw a diamond in the young prisoner, God also sees the value in you and in me despite the wrongs in our past. He does not keep us prisoners of mistakes He has forgiven but knows the value that we have. He sees beyond what we see in ourselves or what those around us see in us. Do not let yourself be affected by the verdicts that those around you place on your life; rather, let God declare your value and let Him have the last word.

God does not keep us prisoners of mistakes He has forgiven but knows the value that we have. He sees beyond what we see in ourselves or what those around us see in us.

The prolonged test that Onesimus had to pass and that many people have to pass in this day and age has to do with past wrongs that still haunt them. A wrong decision, an abortion, a divorce, an argument with a child, a protracted broken relationship with parents, addictions in which many years were lost, and many other mistakes torment many during their times of quiet. Satan will constantly bring past sins onto the board of your mind to constantly create feelings of guilt and shame to dominate your life. His favorite hit song to sing in your ear will be: "Do You Remember What You Have Done?"

Even when God forgave the sins you have confessed, the Devil will remind you of them to poison your emotions and decisions and steal your joy. He is the accuser that places labels.[46]

Isaiah 43:25 tells us that He forgives our sins, and no longer remembers them—what is forgiven will remain forgiven. God does not bring back your sins and wrongs that have been forgiven; the past no longer has power over you. I believe that many people need to forgive themselves for what they have done and not fall into the trap of feeding thoughts about past failures. Falling prey to this trap leads to a loss of spiritual energy that should be used to live an abundant life. My friend, renew your mind constantly with His promises because He forgave you, and you are the righteousness of God in Christ.

"God made him who had no sin to be sin for us, so that in him we might become the righteousness of God."[47]

When the Evil One takes the parchment with past wrongs and waves it in your face to remind you of what you've done, you will have to face him and proclaim the forgiveness that God has granted you.

> To be sure, all of us adults are persons of sorrow, acquainted with guilt. We all have shadows and skeletons in our backgrounds. But listen, there is Something bigger in this world than we are and that Something bigger is full of grace and mercy, patience, and ingenuity. The moment the focus of your life shifts from your badness to His goodness and the question becomes not "What have I done?" but "What can He do?" release from remorse can happen; miracle of miracles, you can forgive yourself because you are forgiven, accept yourself because you are accepted, and begin to start building up the very places you once tore down. There is grace to help in every time of trouble. That grace is the secret to being able to forgive ourselves. Trust it, shift the focus of your life from your failure to His gracious ability to bring success out of your failures. That is where the hope is: when the circle of self-concern grows smaller, the circle of divine forgiveness grows larger.[48]

When the Evil One takes the parchment with past wrongs and waves it in your face to remind you of what you've done, you will have to face him and proclaim the forgiveness that God has granted you.

Onesimus became a true believer and collaborated with the apostle Paul who became involved in the church in Colossi. Some historians use the writings of Ignatius from the year AD 110 to say that after the death of Pastor Timothy, Paul's disciple, Onesimus was active in the church in Ephesus, eventually becoming a bishop in Ephesus. Of course, researchers have no way to know with certainty this Onesimus mentioned as a bishop was the former slave, but we do know that God specializes in picking up the pieces of a person's life and makes something beautiful out of them.

Our lives are somewhat similar to the life of Onesimus because we also have illusions that fall apart; we also have to pass tests, correct mistakes, seek to understand divine appointments and changes in situations, and make life-changing decisions. In this whole palette of external events and internal experiences, God is working on us to make us become trophies for His greatness and glory. He does not abandon any of us but sees the value of the diamond beyond the mistakes or difficult moments in life.

Reflection Group Questions

1. What are some of people's greatest illusions in the pursuit of happiness? What are some of the most common invisible prisons where people find themselves? Which ones did you directly experience? How did you work to change and overcome them?

2. Describe a situation in your life when God orchestrated a divine appointment. How did you know that God was the One leading the way? What did you learn as a result of this experience?

3. How did Jesus cleanse the parchment charging you of sins? What do you do when the Devil brings these accusations to your mind again?

4. How can you fulfill your role as a mediator for those around you in a practical way? What strategies do you use? What elements or experiences do you draw upon to accomplish this?

5. The test of labels is one of the most common tests you will encounter. What can you do to avoid being influenced by negative labels placed by others? How can you avoid placing labels on others?

CHAPTER THREE

The Mind,
the Great Battlefield

Your battles inspired me—not the obvious material battles but thosethat were fought and won behind your forehead.   – James Joyce

"The weapons we fight with are not the weapons of the world. On the contrary, they have divine power to demolish strongholds. We demolish arguments and every pretension that sets itself up against the knowledge of God, and we take captive every thought to make it obedient to Christ."   – 2 Corinthians 10:4-5 (NIV)

THE LOUVRE MUSEUM in France, the largest and best-known art museum in the entire world, attracts approximately 10 million people per year. These visitors come from all over the world to see the famous works of art, including the *Mona Lisa*, the *Venus de Milo*, the *Winged Victory of Samothrace*, and many other masterpieces. The *Mona Lisa* was painted by Leonardo Da Vinci between 1503 and 1506 and has since increased in value from year to year.

The painting's current worth is difficult to estimate. Some say that it could be sold at auction for at least 750 million dollars; others have estimated up to 2.5 billion dollars—an amount that could pay some of France's indebtedness. Impressive, right?

In 1911, the Louvre museum staff hired 32-year-old Vicenzo Peruggia to manufacture glass cases to be placed over the famous works of art so that the myriad of visitors would not touch them and cause damage. As Vicenzo worked, he became so enamored with the famous *Mona Lisa*, one of the Louvre's most significant attractions, that he stole it. All of France was in a state of alert as 60 detectives searched ceaselessly for the missing painting.[49]

He hid the painting in the storage room of his apartment, where he kept it for approximately two years, hoping that all would be forgotten. After two years, Vicenzo took the *Mona Lisa* to Italy, hoping to sell it to an art gallery in Florence. As he was about to complete the transaction, the Italian art dealer, Alfredo Geri, realized that this was the missing painting from France. He contacted the police and, thus, the painting was recovered. The Louvre Museum welcomed back the *Mona Lisa* on January 4, 1914, three years after its disappearance. Thus, Vicenzo went down in history as the biggest art thief in the whole world.

That stolen painting episode is somewhat of an analogy to our souls. Life can be compared to a museum or an art gallery displaying different values or talents that have been created and placed there by the Great Artist, God. Their purpose is to bring us joy, value, fulfillment, and recognition from those around us.

For example, a sharp mind is a great treasure that the Great Artist has placed in many people's lives. Others have the relational skill of connecting people. Perhaps someone is an introvert who can deeply analyze people and things at first glance, or others might have a unique ability to bring a positive spirit in the lives of those around them. The ability to make money, or other talents with which a person is gifted, were sown there by the Great Artist.

Some people look in admiration at your talents and abilities and say, "I wish I could be like you," and others admire them from a distance without saying anything. Another category consists of those who look at the assets in your life and envy them; others do not even want to acknowledge them.

Usually, people will exhibit different behaviors regarding your talents or values in your life, but don't forget that treasure hunters will always look at true treasures the way Peruggia's eyes looked at that painting.

Jesus said, *"The thief comes only to steal and kill and destroy. I came that they may have **life** and have it abundantly."*[50] In the Greek, two words are used to mean "life." One, *bios*, refers to biological life, and the other, *zoe*, refers to spiritual life within us. In this verse, Jesus refers to zoe when using the word "life"; He referred to the spiritual life within man. His goal is that every human being might experience *zoe*, a plentiful spiritual life to influence the other areas of life as well. On the other hand, the Thief's (the Devil's) aim is to steal and destroy the abundant life from within man, making him live a meaningless life of sorrow and poverty that would effect a person's material life as well.

Therefore, the treasures in your life, whether spiritual in nature, ideas, influence, family, material or of any other nature, are under attack by the Evil One who wants to steal, control and destroy them. They are like lands that the Great Artist gave you in order to bring you great joy and fulfillment; however, they are constantly under the attack of the Devil, who seeks to conquer and master them.

God, the Great artist, put values and skills in your life, but the Thief wants to steal and master them.
Guard your treasures!

The life of the prophet Elijah from the Old Testament reminds us of some treasures that the Enemy wanted to conquer, control, or destroy. Elijah's experience sheds light on our lives and helps us understand what some of the treasures are that are under attack.

What happened at that time? A little political and historical context will help explain the situation and provide a better understanding of Elijah's circumstances. King Ahab, who led Israel, married Jezebel from country of Sidon. As with every marriage, partners bring baggage with them—whether these encumbrances are material, cultural, spiritual, or of any other nature. Ahab's choice for his wife brought the culture and idols from her country to Israel and, over time, created a pagan religious institution, which she advanced and implemented through propaganda. This religion was created by the human mind, with nothing supernatural about it. Thus, in Israel, Jezebel augmented a slow move from worshiping Jehovah to Baal worship.

The altars and monuments of faith reminding the people of God's divine intervention built in those key periods by God's people were torn down. The spiritual state of the nation was like an altar in ruins. In this context, the prophet Elijah appeared on the society scene, bringing a message of punishment for the whole nation to King Ahab because he had strayed from true faith and had implemented idolatry.

Elijah warned the king... *"there shall be neither dew nor rain these years, except by my word,"*[51] and then he left.

For three and a half years, the sky was locked and not even a drop of rain fell to the ground. As an agrarian society, the people depended on the rain for their harvest, and this punishment soon began to affect them. Those years brought great sorrow and poverty to the whole population.

After that time, the prophet Elijah appeared again, reminding them that the sorrow that they were experiencing resulted from the fact that they had strayed from God. He called the people and the idolatrous priests to the mountain for a test to show who was the true God.

The ritual Baal's priests followed was a dizzying affair that led them to lose consciousness as they begged Baal to fulfill their request—to no avail. Upon Elijah's prayer, the fire came down from the sky and consumed the offering. Thus, the test proved who the true God was.

Those in attendance yearning for something real as opposed to a religious system created by humans thirsty for power, understood the miracle that had taken place at this demonstration. Elijah destroyed the elite of the religious institution created by Queen Jezebel, killing the priests. Kind of a tragic episode, right?

Had I been part of that society, I think I would have rather not seen what happened to the idolatrous priests.

The Battleground

After the mass extermination of Jezebel's prophets on Mount Carmel, the queen, who was at the top of the religious pyramid, sent a threatening message to Elijah, warning, "You killed my priestly elite and destroyed my religious structures. By this time tomorrow, I will do the same to your life."

Queen Jezebel was known for her barbaric methods of killing people and the cruelty she used to attain her goals. That threat, together with her cruel acts, created some horrific images in Elijah's mind that began to terrify him. This threat was not part of a game; simply put, the country's biggest demon had risen up and was now chasing him. Jezebel's message was like a hammer hitting a thin mirror.

The threat threw Elijah from the peak of victory to the abyss of despair. Dwelling on her words, he began to run for his life. As he ran, he ruminated more on the queen's threatening words. In his fear, his imagination began running wild.

Her message began to descend deeper and deeper into his soul like a spike being driven deeper with each blow of the hammer, becoming unmovable. That day-long run had physically exhausted him, and the thoughts rolling through his mind at an astonishing speed terrified him even more, until he stopped and said:

"It is enough; now, O LORD, take away my life, for I am no better than my fathers."[52]

The poet, John Milton, said, "The mind is its own place, and in itself, can make a heaven of hell, a hell of heaven."[53] There is a difference between the information that goes into a person's mind and the information that the mind amplifies.

The mind is like a land where some ideas come in, others are born and grow, and when they are fed and watered, they may develop at lightning speed. They are helped along by the imagination, analogies, and correlation, and then begin to give birth to and develop other ideas. They begin to conquer lands and take root there.

The mind can be likened to a mill. The information contained in the mill of the mind will be ground up and analyzed. What the mind's mill grinds will affect your emotions, experiences and direction in life. How you feel might be the product of what your mind consumes. Be attentive to the thoughts that enter your mind; that you turn from one side to another and foster because they will bring a certain mood and will shape your life. *"Be careful how you think; your life is shaped by your thoughts."*[54] When you feel sorrowful and despondent, check on the information that you recently deposited in your mind. Martin Luther was credited with saying, "You cannot stop birds from flying over your head, but you can keep them from building a nest in your hair."

Be careful how you think; your life is shaped by your thoughts.

The apostle Paul said,

> *"The weapons we fight with are not the weapons of the world. On the contrary, they have divine power to demolish strongholds. We demolish arguments and every pretension that sets itself up against the knowledge of God, and we take captive every thought to make it obedient to Christ."*[55]

When Paul wrote these words to the church in Corinth, the people understood what a stronghold was because most ancient regions had fortresses. Even the city of Corinth developed based on the Citadel of Acrocorinthus, which was 1886 feet tall.[56]

Strongholds were fortresses strategically positioned at the tops of hills and, in the event of war, the citizenry could take refuge there. The rule was clear for every person in that time—whoever controlled the stronghold controlled the city because the one who is strategically positioned at a high point has power over those who approach and try to scale its walls or usurp its territories.

This stronghold strategy is also the Enemy's method. He plants thoughts in people's minds, and when fed, these thoughts can become the strongholds that direct their actions. These strongholds composed of ideas, arguments, and pretensions that are against God must be torn down. Each thought, which is a seed of the Enemy, must be taken captive and brought into obedience of before Christ; the seed must not be allowed to develop and grow. The battle is at the level of the mind.

Jezebel's threatening words got into Elijah's mind, and aided by images of her cruel methods, his mind began to build scenarios and a stronghold of fear began to direct his emotions and decisions, causing him to want to die.

I remember conversing with an elderly lady who told me she had a romantic relationship with a young man in her youth that did not end well. The relationship wounded her deeply, causing her to reject all men. Once she began feeding that hurt with other ideas and scenarios, it became a strong fortress that remained in her mind for her entire life.

When I spoke with her toward the end of her life, she told me that she would have liked to have children and grandchildren, but she was unable to turn a blind eye to the negative experience. "Perhaps I would have done things differently now," she said. "I would have tried to get past what had happened. I know other people who went through sorrows in relationships and were able to discount those situations, marry, and be happy. I allowed myself to be overtaken by a failure that I allowed to dominate my life."

If you allow failure, sorrow, worry, deceit, lacks, sadness or betrayal to nest in the land of your mind and feed them, this negativity will strengthen and develop strongholds that master your emotions, decisions, and the direction of your life.

I have met people who were living under an excessive and unhealthy amount of worry, allowing the stronghold of worry to develop in their mind. Others are led by the whip of their sexual instincts that push them in all directions to fulfill their cravings and are unable to control themselves. Others are led by greed, and nothing satiates them. Their fortress of greed is a tool the Devil uses to fool them. They want to gather and gather and run until they are in the grave, still not having had enough money or material possessions. Others are tortured by all sorts of dark thoughts tormenting them inside.

> "But I am afraid that just as Eve was deceived by the serpent's cunning, your minds may somehow be led astray from your sincere and pure devotion to Christ"
>
> (2 Corinthians 11:3 NIV).

The apostle Paul told the faithful that he had a certain fear that "the snake in the garden of Eden" might deceive them too—the way the serpent had deceived Eve. The Devil's goal is to destroy thinking that is clean and faithful to Christ.

These strongholds composed of different ideas, arguments, repeated stories or habits are the central point of the spiritual war that the Christian leads. Jesus defeated the forces of darkness, and our access to the Father is open. However, the means the Devil uses to deceive people is by creating ideological strongholds in the mind through trickery and doubt.

The apostle Paul reminds us that we are gifted with strong spiritual weapons and that, in order to take down these strongholds formed by ideas that are raised against knowledge of God, every thought must be made a servant of obedience to Christ. Every believer's responsibility is to detect the strongholds of the Evil One, and with the aid of the Holy Spirit, destroy them.

In her book, *Think, Learn, Succeed,* Dr. Caroline Leaf highlights the following fact:

> Powerful technologies have established that these biophysical correlates of memory, which are called memory engrams, our thoughts, have real, solid, physical representation and are made of proteins. These thoughts keep changing in response to our thinking; we essentially control our ability to build thoughts, and this building allows us to determine what our brains look like and what we want—and need—in our heads.[57]

The greatest battle is for the strongholds built in man's mind.

Some time ago, Eric Klinger, a psychologist from the University of Minnesota, performed an experiment regarding "bad" thoughts that invade the mind. He reached the conclusion that within a 16-hour day, approximately 500 unintentional thoughts invade a person's mind that last for approximately 14 seconds. The majority of these thoughts have to do with daily life, 18 percent were unacceptable, uncomfortable or politically incorrect—mean thoughts, and the remaining 13 percent of these thoughts were out of character, ugly, and shocking—perverse, criminal thoughts.[58]

For approximately 116 minutes per day, evil thoughts show up at the mind's door, want to enter the mind and set up camp there. Our responsibility is to check each thought that comes and to *"take captive every thought to make it obedient to Christ."*[59] The mind is a treasure that God gave you and one that you must guard, not allowing the Evil One's seeds or ideas to nest there, rather allowing only good thoughts to develop.

I must also mention the fact that each of us was born into a sinful nature, and some have lived in this nature for 15, 30, 60 years, while certain paradigms of thought or strongholds were created at the level of the mind and became a part of our life. Once we were transferred into God's kingdom or were born again, those strongholds were not eliminated but are still present and active. Each believer's responsibility, with the aid of the Holy Spirit, is to detect and tear down the strongholds that might be erroneous paradigms of thought, bad habits, or sinful tendencies.

Each believer's responsibility, with the aid of the Holy Spirit, is to detect and tear down the unacceptable strongholds in the mind.

How Can I Defend My Mind?

"Take up the shield of faith, with which you can extinguish all the flaming arrows of the evil one."[60]

Imagine in ancient times when a region would be attacked by an enemy army using a scorched-earth type of campaign. The archers would tip their arrows with a concoction of tar, set them on fire, and using their bows, aim the arrows toward that land. Imagine thousands or tens of thousands of arrows flying at one time and some piercing the thatched roofs of the villagers' houses, setting buildings on fire; others would set fire to fields of crops, thus destroying entire lands.

The Evil One uses this same type of devastation campaign against our minds. The burning arrows are ideas seeking to burn down lands in the mind, to destroy and conquer. These can be arrows of worry, insults, gossip, media attacks, and many others meant to inflict harm.

The protection that we have against these arrows is the "shield of faith which will block the arrows and extinguish the burning arrows of the Evil One." The ancient shields were made of bent wood and covered with layers of leather. Each soldier was responsible for the upkeep of his shield to maintain its efficiency in battle. Since the leather would dry over time, each soldier was responsible for applying oil to his shield as protection against the burning arrows that would strike it. A dry shield could easily light on fire, but one that was rubbed in olive oil prevented the shield from catching fire and burning. Isaiah presents the image of the soldiers applying oil to their shields before war: *"They set the tables, they spread the rugs, they eat, they drink! Get up, you officers, oil the shields!"*[61]

For a soldier in God's army, the *oil* represents the Holy Ghost putting a fresh anointing on the shield of faith. From a spiritual point of view, when the shield of faith dries out, it can easily be lit up by the fire created by the Evil One's arrows. When the shield of faith is anointed by quiet meditation on the words of the Bible, by prayer as dialogues, by fasting and discoveries in the spiritual world, among many others, a fresh anointing is applied. Each soldier in God's army is responsible to have a fresh anointing over his faith and life.

Each soldier is responsible for having
a fresh anointing over his faith and life.

Another aspect to consider when defending the mind from the Evil One's attacks is proper food and drink.

The angel of the LORD came back a second time and touched him and said, "Get up and eat, for the journey is too much for you." So, he got up and ate and drank. Strengthened by that food, he traveled forty days and forty nights until he reached Horeb, the mountain of God."[62]

The hero Elijah was sleeping after a long day of running and building the stronghold of fear in his mind. While the prophet slept, the angel approached him, put on his apron and chef's hat, and prepared warm food for him to eat and water to drink. The food contained nutrients that would feed his body and help him reach Mount Horeb that was approximately 400 miles away.

The food that the angel prepared was God's idea because angels are an extension of God's arm in action. All of us need food for our minds, which consume information upon information daily. When we allow negative information such as *Jezebel's message* to enter our minds, our spirit will be affected adversely. However, when we consume the food that God prepared for us, we will be strengthened to move forward.

Jesus said: *"I am the Bread and the Water of life. If anyone eats of this bread, he will live forever. If anyone thirsts, let him come to me and drink."*[63] This food, which is Christ, can be found in the Bible. I have had periods in life when a thick layer of dust accumulated on my Bible and the soul's dialogue with the heaven was nonexistent. I also noticed during this time that guidance at the spiritual level was difficult. I experienced a spiritual drying out because I was not taking in His messages intended to feed my mind and soul in a positive way. I do not know how your life is, but I think that each of us needs to take in more of His promises. The *zoe* life, the abundant life, comes from taking in the menu that He has prepared for us.

> *The zoe life, the abundant life, comes from taking in the menu that He has prepared for us.*

Another important aspect to defending the mind is maintaining peace.

"Do not be anxious about anything, but in every situation, by prayer and petition, with thanksgiving, present your requests to God. And the peace of God, which transcends all understanding, will guard your hearts and your minds in Christ Jesus" (Philippians 4:6-7 NIV).

I know people who have told me that they would feel extremely tired at night. "I was unable to sleep all night; my thoughts were racing in from every direction—as though an actual war was taking place in my mind. I simply could not sleep." They would lie in a comfortable bed to rest and sleep until the morning, but in spite of their fatigue, they awakened in the morning even more tired than when they went to bed the night before. The body was ready for sleep, but the mind tossed and turned the thoughts from one side to another, trying to find solutions or answers to various situations. Worry, sorrow, or other emotions of that sort often take hold of people's minds and keep them awake through the night.

The apostle Paul says that the worries of the mind must be surrendered before God through prayer, requests, and thanks; then His peace comes and sets over your mind. The process is supernatural—an exchange at the spiritual level. You give Him, the All-Powerful One, your pain and worry; He gives you His peace. At the same time, He reminds you that all things are working in your favor.

"In my favor? Mine?"

Yes, absolutely!

"And we know that for those who love God all things work together for good, for those who are called according to his purpose."[64]

According to this verse, anything that happens in your life—even if you do not understand it at the time or if it seems to be against you—if you love Him, then all things are working in your favor. When you begin to accept whatever God allows in your life as being part of His divine plan, you will gain a sense of peace and calm in your mind, regardless of what is happening around you even if you don't understand the reasons why.

If you are now going through a situation that you do not understand and see that circumstances or people are against you, pray this prayer with me:

God, I don't understand why I am going through this difficult time, but I ask that You turn the situation back in my favor. Give me peace of mind, strength to overcome the current difficulties and help me to believe that all things are working in my favor. I thank You for being all-powerful and for helping me. Amen.

May I say that God listens to prayers that come from the heart's sigh, the mind's wordless scream, or the prayer said aloud. He listens, and He answers.

Caves as Traps

The prophet Elijah finished eating what the angel-cook had prepared for him, and he began to run for another 40 days until he reached Mount Horeb. There he hid in a cave so no one would find him.

The nation was about to experience a spiritual awakening after the demonstration of faith on Mount Carmel. The nation had been moved to action, though their leader had suddenly left his ministry. He was emotionally fragile, unstable, hiding in the cave of loneliness, isolated and discouraged because of fear, wounds, and threats.

I have seen that same attitude of withdrawal, isolation, and loneliness in the lives of many people who had previously been used as God's tools to lift up and encourage others. For many who had been hurt emotionally, the cave of loneliness and isolation became the emotional shell in which they took refuge. We often hide in this place to protect ourselves and to disconnect from what took place. We isolate ourselves to dress our wounds in hopes that everything would somehow end or be forgotten with the passage of time. Certainly, loneliness in such conditions is not good.

In her book, *Braving the Wilderness*, Brené Brown shared the following:

> In a meta-analysis of studies on loneliness, researchers found the following: Living with air pollution increases your odds of dying early by 5 percent. Living with obesity, 20 percent. Excessive drinking, 30 percent. And living with loneliness? It increases our odds of dying early by 45 percent.[65]

The cave of loneliness, which seems like a safe place, unexpectedly shortens the lives of those who hide in its apparent comfort. I believe that people retreat into different "caves" for reasons that only each person understands best, and they are 100 percent right. I do not dispute that what happened to you was likely terrible, but the problem is that if you stay in the cave of isolation and loneliness for too long, that solitude becomes a killer. I urge you to come out of there as fast as you can.

That same place in the caves of loneliness and isolation is also the place of much potential. Some sources claim that Africa is the land with the most wealth—even more than America, Europe or Asia. Still, the continent remains the poorest land because its resources are not being tapped and utilized. Likewise, those who have isolated themselves have removed their talents and refuse to communicate or exercise the skills they possess.

Those who have isolated themselves have taken talents and skills not being used and refuse to communicate or exercise the skills they possess.

Toward the end of my teenage years, I remember some friends who were spelunking guides in a few caves. I still have a vivid memory of standing before a cave opening that would take approximately three hours to cross. We would literally enter one side of the mountain and come out on the other side. The first steps involved descending approximately 25 feet into the mountain on a somewhat rickety ladder that shook at each connection. When my turn came, I stared at the mouth of the cave that was merely a hole. I contemplated stepping on that rickety ladder that I had heard creak as my friends had descended, wondering exactly how sturdy it was. As I gazed at the mountain whose peak I could not see, my body began to go into alert mode, pumping adrenaline into my blood. For some of my friends, traversing that cave was really fun; for me, it was a real, undeniable danger.

At the entrance, the cave guide both instructed us and warned us. He basically said that it was very dark and humid in the cave; therefore, flashlight batteries would die quickly. In lieu of flashlights, we were given gas lamps to see in the pitch-black darkness. The small lamps were convenient to carry, but I quickly found they cast eerie shadows in dark corners as they illuminated the projections of rocks from the walls that sometimes appeared distorted and unreal. The guide instructed us to stay together and to keep the noise down because the sounds could cause some loose stones to fall. At that point I realized that the three hours of caving I was facing, sometimes crawling from one gallery to the next would be terrifying for me.

When I finally came out safely on the other side of the mountain, I realized that if I had been alone in the cave and wandering its labyrinth, the more difficult it would have been for me to find my way out—especially being so inexperienced. I will even admit that after being guided through that cave, which was designed for professionals, was the last one I went into. No more!

Likewise, when a person advances further into the cave of loneliness, isolation, rebellion, vengeance, to name only a few, or when he/she allows the strongholds created in the mind by *Jezebel's messages* to develop, the harder it will be to get out of those mazes.

For those who are in different caves, exactly what the guide told me at the entrance to that cave is taking place. With no natural light, the shadows will project strangely on the walls of the cave, and reality will become distorted. When you have withdrawn into a cave to ruminate over pain, negative messages, or untrue stories, a distorted reality will be strongly projected on the walls of your soul. Some shadows projected on the walls of the soul will look hideous, and the more you take them in, the farther they will take you from reality.

I know a few people who have created an untrue, but

favorable to them, story in their minds, which they have repeated, told, and relived in their minds and emotions until they believed their narrative to be true. No one could get an accurate story from them any longer. The story took root in the land of their minds and formed a strong bunker there. When I spoke to them, I was truly surprised how they could be so convinced of the truth that was such an untruth. In the various caverns where our souls retreat, the strongholds of a lack of faith and untruth develop best and fastest.

When those who experience different caves in their souls look at the Bible's promises through their spiritual eyes, they see the extraordinary truths contained in its pages:

- I can do all things through Christ who strengthens me.
- I am more victorious through He who loved me.
- I am blessed.
- All things work together in my favor.

But when they look with human eyes at the projections of faithlessness on the walls of the soul, they start to see a reality different than the one presented by the Bible. A true battle takes place at the level of the mind and soul between believing what God says versus believing what we see around us.

A true battle takes place at the level of the mind and soul between believing what God says versus believing what we see around us.

What Are You Doing Here, Elijah?

There he came to a cave and lodged in it. And behold, the word of the LORD came to him, and he said to him, "What are you doing here, Elijah?"

He said, "I have been very jealous for the LORD, the God of hosts. For the people of Israel have forsaken your covenant, thrown down your altars, and killed your prophets with the sword, and I, even I only, am left, and they seek my life, to take it away."

And he said, "Go out and stand on the mount before the LORD."

And behold, the LORD passed by, and a great and strong wind tore the mountains and broke in pieces the rocks before the LORD, but the LORD was not in the wind. And after the wind an earthquake, but the LORD was not in the earthquake. And after the earthquake a fire, but the LORD was not in the fire. And after the fire the sound of a low whisper. And when Elijah heard it, he wrapped his face in his cloak and went out and stood at the entrance of the cave. And behold, there came a voice to him and said, "What are you doing here, Elijah?"[66]

The way God speaks to Elijah is a lesson in counselling for all of us. Some of us would have expected that God would have spoken to him in the form of thunder to terrify him or in the form of fire to burn him for running away and abandoning the ministry. Instead, God approached him and spoke to him in a calm and delicate way. When people who are hurt and have withdrawn to the cold confines of a cave, they need a calm conversation to warm up their chilled and isolated souls. After mistakes, pain and loneliness, each of us needs encouragement and uplifting when we are in such places. Likewise, when approaching someone who is in such a situation, calmly approach the person with the purpose of encouraging.

God tells Elijah to come out of the cave and talk in the open because the deeper he goes in the cave, the darker it is. The projections on the soul's walls are more unreal, making it difficult for His voice to be heard.

"What are you doing here, Elijah?" He asks. "What are you doing hiding in this cave? I have given you so many qualities, and you have been victorious against the current. You abandon everything because of some threats and you run?!"

Likewise, He approaches our souls when they are taking refuge in all kinds of caves, whether it's the cave of victimization, of sorrow, of regret, of accusations in the mind, or verdicts and labels that others have put onto our lives, and He lovingly asks, "What are you doing here, my child? What are you doing here in this state? My goal for you is *zoe*—a life of abundance. I put dreams in you that you can fulfill, new ideas, talents, and you have retreated into a cold, dark cave?"

Elijah's answer came from the projections from the cave's walls: "I am the only one left fighting for You, and they seek to take my life."

God answered, "The truth is that I have another 7000 men just like you who serve Me; you are not the only one."

Jezebel's trap for Elijah had the purpose of convincing him to withdraw from the ministry. The paradigm of the trap that snared Elijah followed a definite pattern:

Wounded → Retreated to different caves → Burying the charisma → Self-imposed exclusion from the ministry

Unfortunately, I have seen many people fall into this paradigm trap and withdraw from doing anything in His kingdom, exactly when they could have fulfilled their youthful dreams of serving God. Many Elijahs of our present time have fallen into Jezebel's trap of withdrawal, abandonment of service, or non-exercise of charisma.

The paradigm trap is made of: wounding → Withdrawal into different caves → the burial of charisma → Self-imposed exclusion from ministry

The apostle Paul tells us:

> *"For this reason I remind you to fan into flame the gift of God, which is in you through the laying on of my hands, for God gave us a spirit not of fear but of power and love and self-control."*[67]

The charisma God placed in your life must be sparked by

allowing it to manifest. Exercising your charisma means coming out of your cave and beginning to serve others. The gift received is for lifting up those around you first, and when doing so, you automatically uplift yourself too. Encouragement comes from the fact that the spirit that God put in your life is not a spirit of fear, but of power, of love, and of discipline.

How Do I Get Out of the Cave?

One of the great problems that people in the caves have is that they want to fix their symptoms, but they do not want to forsake the habits created to address the reasons that brought them there. Treating the symptoms of a disease but not wanting to excise the root will not work. The first factor that will help us leave the various caves or even refrain from entering them is facing situations with the Bible.

When God asked Elijah, "What are you doing here?" He then allowed His prophet to speak his point of view and air out his emotions. Of course, certain parts of his story were not legitimate, but God allowed him to speak then offered to correct his point of view. "I have another 7000 people just like you." Each of us needs to be in the presence of His Word to calibrate our thoughts, imaginations, arguments, and stories.

"For the word of God is alive and active. Sharper than any double-edged sword, it penetrates even to dividing soul and spirit, joints and marrow; it judges the thoughts and attitudes of the heart."[68]

"If you hold to my teaching, you are really my disciples. Then you will know the truth, and the truth will set you free."[69]

For me, the Bible is God's love letter, in which He tells me, "I love you." When I sit and read it, it tells me where I am wrong. I liken reading the Word of God to being in a courtroom where my feelings and the thoughts of my heart are analyzed and judged. I have noticed that I have avoided some cave traps or was able to get out of some when I was lost in their mazes by permanently analyzing situations through the light of His Word that confronted my thoughts and feelings.

Avoiding the cave traps or coming out of certain mazes in which the soul is sometimes immersed happens only when the believer allows the Word to confront his thoughts and feelings.

Another aspect to consider is the fact that Elijah receives a ministry—a project that animates him and takes him out of the place where he was.

"And the Lord said to him, "Go, return on your way to the wilderness of Damascus. And when you arrive, you shall anoint Hazael to be king over Syria. And Jehu the son of Nimshi you shall anoint to be king over Israel...."[70]

The ministry that Elijah received was meant to be of national and international impact. He had to anoint the next king of Syria and the next king of Israel—before the fall of Jezebel. I note that God does not abandon people who are going through the valleys of despair because He still has work to do through them. The ministry that Elijah received was meant to energize him and take him out of that cave, but he had to decide between the strongholds of his mind and the project that lay ahead. Most of the time, the mind's imagination kills the vision that God gives us while it's still an embryo.

Likewise, each of us need projects to inspire us and take us out of the caves where we often find ourselves. My friend, what is your ministry? If you don't have such a project, I want to remind you that Elijah received that ministry while sitting in the presence of the Lord. The same can happen to you.

Often, the mind's imagination kills the vision that God gives you while it's still an embryo.

Thirdly, Elijah received a new friend.

"and Elisha the son of Shaphat of Abel-meholah you shall anoint to be prophet in your place."[71]

Elijah's new friend would start as his servant, then his disciple, and finally a friend with whom he would share many burdens.

Elijah would often seek his protégé's counsel. That Elisha would take over Elijah's ministry in the country was no surprise.

Our society nowadays is crowded with many busy people, but what many are missing is the presence of true friends—friends who can be a support in hard times, with whom they can consult on life's dilemmas and who can, at the same time, correct them.

"Faithful are the wounds of a friend, but deceitful are the kisses of an enemy."[72]

We need friends who love the Truth and who are ready to constantly confront our wrong ideas or actions. With such friends, we will avoid going deep into various caves.

The greatest battles are fought over the territories of your mind and mine. Whoever wins battles builds different strongholds and leads from there. Our lives are directed from the control tower, which is the mind. Likewise, your spiritual ministry is influenced by the ideas developed in the mind. The apostle Paul reminds us that the mind must be renewed to please God.

"Do not conform to the pattern of this world, but be transformed by the renewing of your mind. Then you will be able to test and approve what God's will is—his good, pleasing and perfect will."[73]

Reflection Group Questions

1. How can you guard your mind in a practical way so that the Evil One cannot build up the strongholds of fear, faithlessness and sorrow?

2. How can you dismantle the incorrect thought paradigms that have developed in your mind over time? What do you to prevent them from returning?

3. What are the strongest arrows that have attacked your mind lately? How were you able to stop them using the shield of faith?

4. Into what cave do you tend to retreat most often? What are some practical steps you can take to avoid entering various caves?

5. To what extent are your friends a source of support for your spiritual life? How can you also be a friend who uplifts others in the life of faith in a practical way?

CHAPTER FOUR

The Value of a Scar

"From every wound there is a scar, and every scar tells a story. A story that says, I survived."

– Fr. Craig Scott

"When he was at table with them, he took the bread and blessed and broke it and gave it to them. And their eyes were opened, and they recognized him. And he vanished from their sight." — Luke 24:30-31 (ESV)

IN THE FIFTEENTH century, a memorable contest was held in China for plate and porcelain designers. This contest motivated many, and the winner would be promoted within the ranks of porcelain specialists and would become renowned in society. Many practiced the art with great mastery and impatiently awaited the contest to show their creations and become winners.

Tradition has it that a young man named Li, like many others, dreamed of winning the renowned contest being held during that time. For months he worked on his piece—a porcelain plate in an original design, decorated differently than anything he had ever seen before. He hoped with all his heart to be chosen as the winner of this eminent contest.

The night before the contest, while he was wiping and nervously examining the porcelain plate for one last time, he accidentally dropped the plate, which shattered into pieces. He couldn't believe what had just happened. As he stood staring at the shattered porcelain plate, tears began to flow from his eyes like a river.

In that moment, his dreams shattered.

With his head bowed and tears streaming down his chin, he told his parents what had happened. His parents, who knew how hard he had worked on creating that plate and what his dream was, looked at him with a heavy heart. After listening to his sorrow and after long consideration, they decided to give their son all of the gold they had saved. If he melted that gold, he could use the liquid gold to glue it back together piece by piece and restore the porcelain plate to its original beauty. After a hard night of work and after putting the last piece in place, he looked at his creation now with golden veins holding the shattered pieces together.

The next day at the contest, each participant brought his or her porcelain dish before the judges and had to describe each masterpiece's creation and meaning. When young Li brought his porcelain plate full of gold veins, everyone was amazed and interested to hear its story. No one had seen anything like it before. He explained how the original masterpiece was accidentally shattered, but through the kindness of his parents, the pieces were glued back together with gold plus other components, making it even stronger and more valuable.

That year, the young man joined the ranks of famous porcelain artists and became renowned in society. Later on, this art of gluing together the pieces[74] of an object made of ceramic, porcelain, or similar materials Li pioneered became known as *Kintsugi*.

Many people have, at a given time in life, seen their dreams, relationships, or other aspects of life shatter to pieces. Perhaps they wished with every fiber of their being for certain developments to happen in their lives to help them become winners, but events did not go as they had hoped. Those shards of disappointment are, in fact, the wounds or scars in their lives. Each of them has an interesting story that forms part of life's history. Those moments of shock when faced with disappointment or looking at the broken pieces are decisive moments for many. Some decide to pick up the pieces, bury them in the past and give up; others decide that the pieces can be glued together and can become even stronger and more valuable. The latter are those who have left an imprint on history and on the lives of others.

Have you experienced moments when certain aspects or dimensions of your life have shattered? If you look at your past, you can likely identify episodes when certain relationships were broken; perhaps someone hurt you or took advantage of you or perhaps you were even marginalized or excluded.

Perhaps you also worked on the dish of your dreams,

thinking that you would be able to achieve recognition and thus climb the social ladder, but everything shattered. When we scan our past or maybe even our present, we can see the sharp-edged pieces that we no longer know how to touch to avoid being emotionally cut by them or to avoid further breakage.

Life's shards can be glued together
and become even stronger and more valuable.
Those who live and act in this way have left
an imprint on history and on the lives of others.

The Bible always has something to say about shattered dreams, disappointed hearts, deep wounds, jagged scars, and their value.

The two travelers left via the gate of Jerusalem and walked with their heads hanging low. They were deep in thought as they walked in step. At the soul level, they were reliving the previous events that had taken place as fast as a lightning bolt illuminating the dark night. Not even their ability to react had kicked in since the events had taken place much too quickly.

Though restless, the duo was also calm—like being in the eye of a tornado with disaster circling all around. Theirs had been the epitome of excitement, thinking that changes in their country would come since Jesus, the Messiah, had appeared. Now they were on the road of disappointment when what they had imagined and dreamed had drifted away.

Because of His presence, they had planned for the following years. They imagined climbing higher on the social ladder, but now they wandered aimlessly, not knowing what would happen in their lives today...let alone tomorrow. They had simply been thrown from the extremity of excitement to that of desperation. One of the travelers was named Cleopas and his unnamed friend could be me or even you.

Have you ever walked on this road of disappointment where life, friends, dreams, all drifted away in a matter of moments, bringing a bitter taste? If you look inside yourself, you will see various wounds in your soul—some still open and others scarred. If we would sit down for coffee together and you told me about each of your wounds and scars, I feel sure that each has a unique, vivid and detailed story.

The truth is scars are part of the stories of our lives. Positive events remain engraved on our minds, but the negative ones with passionate emotional depth remain acutely imprinted on our souls. We usually do not recall all the details about what was said or how they happened, but we certainly remember our feelings that remain attached to the pains, wounds and scars that we have experienced or continue to experience.

Positive events in life remain engraved in our minds, but the negative ones with strong emotional intensity remain imprinted on our souls much more deeply.

What Happened in the Lives of the Two Travelers?

The 33-year-old rabbi they had been following had excelled in meeting the needs of people. Crowds would gather around Him as He addressed them with strength and charm. He exuded an innate *charisma*, people said. Some He fed, others He healed, and most interesting was His ability in knowing how to respond to the religious leaders, and people liked His intuitive confidence. Thus, the young rabbi, Jesus, struck a chord in the hearts of the masses, and they became attached to him, considering him capable of becoming an emperor. Hope began to rise again in them that a liberator who would free them from Roman rule was among them.

Of course, others had also tried to be revolutionary heroes and had failed, but this rabbi seemed to be totally different. His growing popularity struck a chord of hatred in the politico-religious class. After an evil plan was devised, the leaders unfairly accused the young rabbi, initiated a false and unlawful trial, beat Him half to death, crucified Him, and once He was dead, buried Him.

Certainly, the two travelers' trip from Jerusalem to Emmaus gave them a little time to analyze and examine the facts from one side to another. Cleopas walked with his head down, trying to put each event in its place to see what could have possibly gone wrong. They talked and processed the events weighing on their heart, like the strike of a hammer on a porcelain plate. They were disappointed that what they had expected to happen did not take place. They were expecting that the young rabbi would become the emperor, and those who had followed

Him for three years would become ministers or reach other key leadership positions in their country; however, what they had imagined did not materialize nor would happen now. *The man in whom they had put their hopes was buried.*[75]

The road Cleopas and his friend walked was the road of disappointment.

Disappointment arises from the difference between someone's expectations, the scenario created in his mind, and the reality that occurs. When expectations and life's reality do not coincide, disappointment is born. In relationships with those around us, most disappointments come from the fact that we cannot make people act or react the way we want.

With regard to what we want, disappointment arises when circumstances are not in tandem with what we have in mind. This letdown can lead to an abundance of bitterness in our life. Likewise, discouragement sets into the soul most easily in moments when we analyze life's circumstances based on sensory information that is not as we would wish. When we've removed reliance on faith and His promises from our life's equation, we forget that "He will make all things work for our good."[76]

Sometimes, disappointment also appears because of a demonic attack. When the Devil sets his artillery expressly on a person with the purpose of disqualifying or destroying that person or pushing him away from God's plans, then disappointment will be like a black cloud surrounding him.

"Simon, Simon, Satan has asked to sift each of you like wheat."[77]

God has a Book in which all of your days and mine are written before any of them even take place. *"Your eyes saw my unformed body; all the days ordained for me were written in your book before one of them came to be."*[78]

But we, as people, have our own books with our plans, goals, wishes, revenges, hidden passions, and vices that we live day to day. When the two scripts or narratives do not coincide, a lot of disappointment arises. His plan is good and has the purpose of giving us a future and hope. But when our plans reign, we often go in a costly and painful direction.

Different Pieces

Many aspects of our lives can shatter in the blink of an eye. I don't believe this concept is foreign to anyone who has lived on earth.

Some are disappointed in love. He fell in love with someone who looked so good, and everything in the relationship was rose-colored. After a year and a half, everything suddenly changed. She removed her mask, and the true portrait was revealed. The initial mask was attractively painted, but the current reality was in stark contrast with what was initially seen.

Others are disappointed in the arena of finance. They expected that numbers would spin faster in their favor in their bank account, but the numbers seem somewhat stubborn. Plans made in their minds or on paper fail to coincide with reality in the bank account. "I can't believe this! Is everything against me?"

Another disappointment for some is their workplace. Their promotion expectations did not match with their boss's, and the atmosphere in the workplace became toxic. The tension can be felt in the air. "How will it end? Will I be fired?"

At some point, each of us will hear the sound of things shattering in one area or another. However, the most important decision is "What do we do with the pieces—the wounds, the shattered dreams or the scars that we bear in life?

Isaiah 61:3 talks about "a spirit of despair" or "a spirit of heaviness" that absorbs energy and spiritual power from man and creates the attitude of a victim devoid of courage. This "spirit of despair," which manifests itself very strongly in today's world, creates a defensiveness in many people.

- Some hide their wounds or scars so that no one will see them. They do not intend to reveal any kind of unfortunate part of their history for anyone.

- Some model their identity after their wounds or scars. They identify with the tragedies they've experienced. In the book of Ruth, because of Naomi's adverse experiences, she tells her neighbors not to call her *Naomi,* which means "pleasant one," but to instead call her *Mara,* which means "bitterness."[79] Naomi's wounds and scars began to define her identity. The Bible never calls her *Mara,* only *Naomi* because God will never name you or identify you based on the wounds or failures you have experienced.

- Others wear their scars like medals, showing others what they have been through and suffered. Despite these difficult times, they came out victorious. Scars are like a type of history of these people's courage and bravery, and they seek attention through them.

- Some become victims after certain events and carry a victim attitude in their souls and minds throughout their entire life. Their every action, thought, and word is passed through the filter of the negative experience they have endured.

In the difficult moments that we sometimes experience, the Devil appears and pushes us down the slope of disappointments. He uses our unexpressed deceptions and weaves in a cloth to catch us, wrap us, and isolate us, making us easy prey. He applies this strategy after unresolved and unexpressed disillusionments.

In her book, *It's Not Supposed to Be This Way*, Lysa Ter-Keurst shares the following thought:

> In the quiet, unexpressed, unwrestled-through disappointments, Satan is handcrafting his most damning weapons against us and those we love. It's his subtle seduction to get us alone with our thoughts so he can slip in whispers that will develop our disappointments into destructive choices.[80]

The ideology that the Devil injects into the minds of some is negativism and pessimism. This strategy has the purpose of coloring our lives in black ink and casting suspicion around God who said:

"Taste and see that the LORD is good...."[81]

"How is God good to me when something like this happens?"

The Devil's thoughts want to put life's disappointments in contrast to God's promises. And even if the trials and difficulties in life are great, and if the Devil wants to make us easy prey, Isaiah 61:3 (NIV) brings a promise full of light:

*"and provide for those who grieve in Zion—to bestow on them a crown of beauty instead of ashes, the oil of joy instead of mourning, and **a garment of praise instead of a spirit of despair**. They will be called oaks of righteousness, a planting of the LORD, for the display of his splendor."*

For those who grieve, I will give them a crown of beauty for ashes, the oil of joy for mourning, and a garment of praise for a spirit of despair.

Sometimes Jesus Looks Different

While Cleopas and his friend walked on, a traveler with his head covered, who was probably wearing a hood as some Hebrew travelers were often dressed, approached them and started conversing with them, asking, "What is the subject of your deep conversation?"

They answered him with a question. "Are you only person visiting in Jerusalem who doesn't know what has recently happened?"

The traveler pretended not to know what they were talking about and asked for explanations. The unrecognizable traveler was Jesus, who had risen from the dead, "But their eyes were prevented from recognizing Him."[82]

Why didn't they recognize him? Because three days prior, the horrible image of the crucifixion they had seen had been imprinted in their minds and had shaken them deeply. Now this hooded stranger didn't even know about the events that had taken place that had rocked the entire metropolis. The One on the cross and the hooded traveler were two contradicting images.

"Their eyes were prevented from recognizing him."

Certainly, God had a role in that non-recognition. These disciples were not the only ones who had trouble recognizing Jesus. Many times, we also have this difficulty because we created ourselves an image of Jesus or of the way He should look and where we might find Him and if, perhaps, He shows up in a different way, we no longer recognize Him.

We've somewhat set our minds to identify only certain aspects that can be connected or be closely tied to a certain person, and everything that is beyond that perimeter is difficult to identify.

Some see God as an old man who walks around in the sky

with His cane, a capricious man who is impossible to get along with. If you somehow err, He will strike you with His cane. Others have an image of a God who has retreated somewhere far away in the cosmos and who has no connection with what is happening in our world.

Another category of people places God on a cross in a window among other trinkets or around their neck on a chain and think they have Him nearby.

One religious man, Saul from Tarsus, also had an idea about God, which was in harmony with his religion, but in contradiction with the Jesus he encountered on the way to Damascus. We create an idea about how God is or should be, and we hold on to that point of view that has been influenced by culture, by those around us, by different events we have experienced and theological trends. If Jesus would come to us in a different form or in a different way than we imagine, would we recognize Him? Often, our eyes are prevented from seeing Him— just as the disciples' eyes were impeded—because of the ideas that we have and that we want to impose on His manifestation.

R. T. Kendall said, "I think one definition of spirituality, then, is 'the ability to close the gap between the time of the Lord's appearance and our being aware that it is the Lord.'"[83]

Often our eyes are prevented from seeing Him—just as the disciples' eyes were impeded—because of the ideas that we have and want to impose on Him.

Scars that Convince

Cleopas and his friend were somewhat surprised that the traveler was not up-to-date on the events that had taken place in recent days. And still He interpreted them as current events through the prism of the prophets of the Old Testament. The discussion was interesting; time flew quickly, and darkness had fallen. They reached their destination, and the hooded traveler pretended to continue walking, but the two asked him to stay with them overnight and to continue their journey the next day.

At dinner, the traveler took the bread and, after praying, broke it, and when He extended it to them, they saw the wounds on His wrists. Like a flashback, those large wounds brought back the images from three days earlier when the Roman hammer powerfully struck the spikes, and they heard the screams from the lungs of those sentenced to death. They saw the three crosses with the crucified men hanging on them.

The wounds they saw on the hands of the person who offered them the bread convinced them that they had been walking with Jesus who had been crucified, and He lived!

"Then their eyes were opened and they recognized him, and he disappeared from their sight."[84]

At the moment of His disappearance, they began to believe that Jesus lived and that they had to return to Jerusalem to tell the disciples that Jesus was alive. Seeing the wounds produced a change in them, and they returned from the road of disappointment back to the path of faith. That encounter transformed them from victims of disillusionment to pioneers of a ministry. Theirs was a ministry to walk and proclaim His resurrection and to lift the other discouraged disciples in Jerusalem. Each physical or emotional scar that you carry has a story to tell. Many people hide their scars under a tattoo, a piece of clothing, or even isolate themselves, forgetting that scars carry with them the story of victory.

"What doesn't kill you makes you stronger."

Scars can make you a victim tortured by a spirit of sorrow or you can use the scars you have to lift others who are on the road of discouragement. Scars are part of your life, and they must become a ministry through which you uplift others. Because of the lessons you have learned, you can help change the path of those who are on the road to desperation and bring them to the road of faith or hope. Thus, scars are a true asset and a real treasure; they play an important role in your ministry.

These still sensitive points in your life must be used very carefully so as not to give others the opportunity to strike you in the same place, but in order to uplift others, you must be vulnerable. After all, these vulnerabilities can only be used once you have overcome your victim mentality. Once you have healed and have faith that God is always good and right, He can use these sensitive points in life to uplift others.

Scars can make you a victim tortured by a spirit of sorrow or you can use the scars you have to uplift others who are on the road of discouragement.

On August 25, 1969, at 7:35 p.m. an eighteen-wheeler hit the Donaldson family's car head on. Hal and his two brothers were catapulted from the car during the accident. Their father, who was 37 years old, died on site; their mother was taken to the hospital, lingering between life and death.

Hal Donaldson was twelve years old when this accident took place. Hal, his two brothers and his sister were taken in by some neighbors until their mother recovered from the multiple fractures and internal injuries.

Those events—the father's untimely death; the hospitalized, recuperating mother; and the resulting poverty the family experienced strongly impacted young Hal. He wished to escape from his life of poverty, earn his own money, and see the world. Being mature for his age, he was often concerned with success and would state: "Someday, I'll give back and help the less fortunate, but my career has to come first."[85]

In my travels, I came face-to-face with people who were suffering and in need: an orphaned boy without shoes, a homeless mother clutching her lifeless child, a Vietnam War vet who had lost his legs, an unemployed man holding a "work-for-food" sign, and more. I could no longer ignore their struggles or escape the guilt of sitting on my hands while the world suffered.[86]

The scar of poverty and the kindness of others toward him helped Hal understand what poverty meant. As a result, he and his siblings decided to create the "Convoy of Hope" non-profit organization designed to help poverty-stricken families and those affected by natural disasters such as hurricanes or tornados by providing food, medication and other goods. Convoy of Hope started with little in 1994, but the organization has now become a movement through which "over 80 million people"[87] were helped.

People do not forget the pain or wounds they have experienced. The resulting impact can constitute the engine that spurs an individual to do something for his neighbor because he understands—both intellectually and emotionally—the troubles of the one going down the road of pain. After all, he has already passed through that place of sorrow.

- The person who has lost a parent or a child can soothe others who have started down the road of tears and are on the verge of losing their mind.

- Once the wounds of a divorce have healed, the person who has gone through it can help someone else traveling that same road who is lost in desperation.

- A person who has declared bankruptcy and recovered from its humiliation will understand and uplift another who is facing this humbling experience.

- Those who have surpassed the deep valleys of suicide can help others who have such inclinations.

The scars that you show those who go down the road of discouragement have the power of changing their path and bringing them to the road of faith or hope.

The Power of Explanation
vs. the Power of Example

"Did not the Messiah have to suffer these things and then enter his glory?" And beginning with Moses and all the Prophets, he explained to them what was said in all the Scriptures concerning himself.[88]

On the road from Jerusalem to Emmaus, the traveler had brought many explanations to the two disciples, showing them from the writings of Old Testament that Christ had to go down that road. Those explanations were not sufficient for the discouraged disciples. They needed something more. The wounds they saw on His hands were the power of example that made them believe that He had indeed risen from the dead.

For those passing through the deep valleys of life, often explanations and theories have limited power. Personal and practical examples, however, have the strength to convince people and engender change. For this reason, share how you overcame your valleys with those who are in the valleys of life. Your personal triumph will become the key for others going through that road to rise.

The apostle Thomas was not present when Jesus first revealed Himself after the resurrection; however, when he met with the other disciples, they explained to him:

> "Thomas, 'we have seen the Lord,'"[89] and they started to explain what had happened.
>
> Thomas said to them, "Unless I see the nail marks in his hands and put my finger where the nails were, and put my hand into his side, I will not believe."[90]

His lack of faith could not be defeated by the others' explanations; he had to be face-to-face with Him who bore the wounds. He needed a reference. Jesus's wounds had the power to transform him from Thomas "the non-believer," to Thomas "the full of faith." The power of example is stronger than the power of explanation.

When people are slammed by different aspects of life or by other people and their lives are shattered, they need an example to show them that "this too shall pass." As in other cases where the pieces were glued back together, the same can be done in their case. Your scars can be an example for those who have little or no hope that anything can be done in their case.

Your scars can be an example for those who have little or no hope that anything can be done in their case.

Hindsight

"Didn't our hearts burn within us as he talked with us on the road and explained the Scriptures to us?"[91]

An analysis of their hearts revealed they were starting to warm up and burn after the journey and after Jesus's disappearance from the table. Until then, they had been unable to notice what was happening around them, but in hindsight, they better understood what had taken place in recent hours.

When you are caught in the midst of life-changing events taking place, you can lack perspective; understanding what God is doing in your life can be difficult. Through faith, you can accept that His plan is good although you cannot always understand what is happening or know in which direction God will take you. Once the season passes and the pieces have been put together, in hindsight, you begin to recognize the imprints of divine intervention.

Joseph's hindsight about events in his life was revealing. He had gone through unimaginable hardships for thirteen years—when his brothers sold him, when he was unfairly accused and when he was thrown in the dungeon. However, at a later time when he became the vice-pharaoh in the Egyptian Empire and the waters had become still, Joseph scanned over the history that took place and affirmed:

"You intended to harm me, but God intended it all for good. He brought me to this position so I could save the lives of many people."[92]

Once everything had passed, he looked at life's events through the lens of providence and divine plan, even if the seasons he had experienced were very difficult.

When you are caught in the storm of events that you cannot understand, sometimes you do not realize that He is developing a much bigger plan than what you can understand at that moment. What those who love God must remember is that a blessed plan is always involved.

Reflection Group Questions

1. For what general reasons does disappointment appear in people's lives? How about in your life? What steps do you take to overcome that disappointment and move on?

2. Describe attitudes you've seen manifesting in people with wounds or scars. What can you do when you recognize them manifesting in your own life?

3. Why are our eyes prevented from seeing Jesus on the road of our lives?

4. How can you use your scars to uplift others?

5. Why is the power of example stronger than the power of explanation? What examples can you provide to support your position? Could you give examples?

CHAPTER FIVE

The Treasure Under the Ruins

"Where is the secret hidden? Who has the key to the treasure box of More?"

– Barbara Brown Taylor

*"The L*ORD* turned to him and said, "Go in the strength you have and save Israel out of Midian's hand. Am I not sending you?"*

"Pardon me, my lord," Gideon replied, "but how can I save Israel? My clan is the weakest in Manasseh, and I am the least in my family."

*The L*ORD* answered, "I will be with you, and you will strike down all the Midianites, leaving none alive."*

– Judges 6:14-16 (NIV)

W HEN ADOLF HITLER came into power after conquering most of Europe and parts of Asia, one of his ambitions was to transform the city of Linz in Austria into a museum that would amaze the entire world. The museum would house Europe's most beautiful paintings, sculptures, and works of art that he had appropriated from the countries he had conquered. He ordered the confiscation of some of the most valuable works of art from museums, churches, universities and transferred into his possession.

According to some sources, Hitler had dreamed of becoming an artist in his youth. He had applied for entrance into Vienna's School of Painting at the Academy of Fine Arts. The aspiring artist was refused not once but twice into the program. He attributed his failure to be accepted to the fact that the admissions committee consisted of unjust Hebrews. The volcano of hatred toward this race started to steam even from his young days.[93]

He confiscated the works of art and hid them in several secret places because his museum project was not yet ready. He stored some of them in secret castles and others in various salt mines in the heart of Austria's mountains. The salt mine in Altaussee,[94] Austria, alone held thousands of priceless works of art. The entrances to the mine holding these treasures hidden underground were blocked with multiple layers of soil and rubble to keep them safe. A multitude of the famous works of art that represented the value, culture and history of Europe laid buried deep underground, and the numerous layers of soil and debris impeded access to them.

This image of these hidden confiscated masterpieces represents the lives of many people. The "treasure" of many skilled and talented people lies sunken or hidden under various layers of ruin. My friend, God put different treasures in your life in order to give you and those around you value and significance; however, these treasures hidden in earthen vessels are often confiscated and buried to prevent them from showing their value and benefits.

When you look at certain people around you, you will perhaps more attentively notice the rubble of preconceived notions or of powerlessness in which they live. Their valuable talents are inactive or lying dormant deep within their being. Nowadays, more than ever we need to bring buried treasures back to their value.

Nowadays we need more than ever to bring buried treasures back to their value.

What eventually happened to the works of art and masterpieces in Altaussee, Austria?

During the war against Hitler, the United Nations, being on the other side of the barricade, agreed that all of these confiscated works of art, which constituted the history, culture and values of Europe, was an unspeakable loss. Therefore, a military unit was assembled with the aim of recovering these priceless treasures. The military unit, called the Monuments Men, consisted of museum directors, historians, and architects. They were not men of combat but scholars who understood the importance of the pieces of art.

During their searches, they found the salt mine in Altaussee with its blocked entrance. After managing to get past the thick layers of rubble and debris acting as barriers to the mine, the searchers found over 4,700 hidden works of art safe within the dark, cool and dry conditions of the mine. Operating with limited resources, the art was carefully removed from the mine, saving some of the cultural and historical treasures of our civilization.[95]

Likewise, in the field of your life, many treasures of priceless value lay buried under multiple layers. Some of those layers, though, have to be swept away. A few of the layers will be easily swept aside; however, layers that are older and have been compacted through the years will have to be demolished because they are stubborn and will not allow you to get past them. Other layers will never disappear but will remain so that the treasures set in contrast with them may shine even brighter.

Suppose you had passed through Altaussee during the time the Monuments Men set about retrieving the art treasures. Suppose you had seen the tunnels firsthand that led to the mine full of soil and rubble chaotically thrown about by the explosions to open them. More than likely, you would not have been at all impressed by what you saw. However, had you known about the treasures hidden beneath that rubble, the wheels of your mind would have started spinning quickly as you started calculating the value hidden there. With your mind's eye, you would have seen the brushes of many artists who had painstakingly worked for months and years on their paintings. You would have pictured the sculptor's chisel working for years on end to bring out the masterpiece hidden within the marble slab. Your mind's eye would have seen the monetary value of what was lying beneath the visible surface.

When you examine your life or the lives of others around you, often you will only see the pile of rubble aimlessly thrown about, creating the impression that nothing of value is hidden beneath its covering. This false illusion—that nothing is good in that life—has been created by the Evil One. This illusion often becomes the norm and even the reality for many. But when you know that God the Creator placed talent, value, and skill into each human, you realize that these useful abilities must somehow be brought to light again.

In the field of your life, there are many treasures of priceless value that lie buried under multiple layers of rubble and ruin. It's time to bring them to light and put them to use.

Life Among the Ruins

In the book of Judges, the life of young Gideon demonstrates in greater detail the concept of the buried treasure and recovering its value. In those days, Gideon lived in extremely difficult circumstances[96] as constant fear and uncertainty loomed in the people's minds as they lived life on high alert. The people's constant apprehension was like a menacing sword positioned above their heads. The citizenry was being invaded by enemy armies who came every year, ransacking their homes of valuables, enslaving any able-bodied people, molesting the women, and inflicting terror and pain on the nation of Israel.

The locals would hide their sacks of grains in the ground, so they would have food supplies to carry them through the following year. Every year during the time when the enemies were known to invade, the families would ready their children to hide in caves and the mountains.

I can almost imagine a five- or a six-year-old girl asking her father, "Do we have to go to that cold, dark place again? I don't like it there; I want to play with the other kids."

And the heartbroken father would answer hopelessly, "Yes, we must leave quickly to be safe. Maybe this year we will flee to the caves for the last time..."

I do not know if these experiences make sense to Generation Z who have been born with a smart device in hand but hiding from the enemy was the reality in those days. You would not want to think about how difficult and hopeless those years must have been for Gideon and his family. Imagine living through countless predators invading your home, taking everything of value you own, destroying everything else, and ruining your future. Imagine starting your life over and repairing the damage. This tragedy took place over and over again for seven years and left deeper and deeper imprints on the lives of the people. The emotional ruin, as well as the spiritual and economic collapse were disastrous both at the national and personal level. No longer could anyone see the light at the end of the tunnel.

In today's society, I have seen the prosperity of many, but most often behind the sparkle and makeup is immeasurable pain. Some dramas are written in books, but most of them are different patterns hidden or embedded in the soul like open wounds or scars that speak of pain.

Try to go beyond the impressive appearances of the people you meet and discreetly apply some healing ointment to soothe their wounds. Even if the predators of Gideon's times came to destroy, most of them would be dressed in modern garb, intending to bring us emotional ruin, to spiritually defraud us and destroy our families—even as they appear to offer an appealing deal. They would likely have no interest in our physical homes or taking our personal property.

Try to go beyond the impressive appearances of the people you meet and discreetly apply some ointment to soothe their wounds.

The writer put young Gideon under the magnifying glass and presented his life from the ruins of that context. The young farmer was in the winepress, a hidden place where he could process the grain and prepare the sacks to then bury them underground. At that time, each grain was important because he knew that as soon as the enemy armies would appear, he would have to go into hiding.

I can imagine his working and wondering, *How long will*

we live like this? When will the menacing sword held over our heads be gone?

The place where he found himself was in the winepress of despair. The sacks that he was filling in order to hide screamed without words about the reality of the fact that they were alone in that state and that God had abandoned them. The desperation that he experienced in his soul was a cruel mockery of all the stories told how God had worked miracles in the nation. Life's ruins often insult God's power at the level of the mind.

So many people today go through this winepress of despair when everything is contrary to His promises. So many can no longer stand the pressure they face daily and are ready to crack from the weight of life. Have you ever been through the press of despair or perhaps you are now going through it?

Like other young people at that time, Gideon was preparing the sacks of grain and was consumed by questions that also seem to echo in our minds.

* *Why can't I live a normal life?*

* *Why can't I have my own house and my own refrigerator?*

* *Why can't I feel secure about tomorrow without fear looming like a merciless sword above me?*

* *Why won't God intervene and do something?*

* *Why do others tell so many stories of miraculous divine interventions in different and even much more difficult situations, but now the heavens stay quiet?*

- *Why does God leave us in these situations and does not hear our prayers or do anything?*

- *I dream of living a normal life, but I wonder why God won't fulfill that dream. I pray and heaven is silent. Why?*

- *Why? Why? Why?*

Do these types of questions knock on your mind's door? Can you hear the echo of the "whys" in your internal universe as well? Have you ever experienced moments when fear, insecurity and sorrow have knocked on your mind's door? Or perhaps you have prayed for a dream you have, and heaven has remained unmoved. It seems like no prayer reaches heaven's gates, and hence, no answer comes from beyond. I have no idea what season of life you are currently facing, but I have noticed on my journey through life that every person has dreams, questions and the wish for Someone to intervene and do something on his behalf.

Each of us has dreams, questions, and the wish that Someone would intervene and do something.

And still, even with all of the questions that young Gideon had in those distressing circumstances, he did what he could. He would prepare his sacks of grains to hide underground. Perhaps Theodore Roosevelt received his inspiration from Gideon when he said, "Do what you can, with what you have, where you are."[97]

This statement shows character and determination because many wait for the wind to push the sails of their ship before starting work. Some are motivated only when circumstances are favorable to their cause, but character and determination are revealed in a person when he does everything he can when the winds of life are against him.

Some are motivated only when circumstances are favorable to their cause, but character and determination are revealed when you do everything you can when the winds of life are against you.

The Changing Dialogue

While Gideon was working at that winepress, the Bible says that an angel started a friendly conversation with him. *An angel?* What type of angel? An angel in disguise! Apparently, the angel was not recognizable as an angel because the Gideon conversed unemotionally with him and expressed his displeasures. To an extent, Gideon shared his dream in the same way two friends would talk over a cup of tea.

By the way, not all angels who come to meet you have white feathers and flap their wings. Conversing with these heavenly messengers may entirely change the course of your life or your

Many people who believe that reaching their dreams is strictly based on material things and cash. "If your wallet is filled," they say, "you will succeed." However, if you don't have the necessary resources for the plan, they see no use in taking any further steps.

I have known people of the faith who subconsciously have latched on to an implanted concept that God can only fulfill certain ideas, dreams, or a specific calling if they possess the necessary resources. This concept is saying that God's power somewhat manifests based on man's resources—a type of limited God. Is that really so?

> One day, after Jesus had taught the ten- to fifteen-thousand people, He healed some of those who were present. The disciples told Him: "Let them go home because it's getting late and they are starving."
>
> Jesus answered the disciples, somewhat brusquely, "You feed them."[102]

He said specifically to Philip, who was from that area, "Where are we to buy bread, so that these people may eat?" He said this to test him, for he himself knew what he would do."[103] In order to resolve the situation, Philip looked into their account [a moneybag at that time] and answered, "Two hundred denarii would not buy enough bread for each of them to have a small piece."[104]

Jesus's question to Philip was, in fact, a test: "How can you solve the problem of feeding ten- to fifteen-thousand hungry people in a deserted place?"

family's life or even your nation's history. Having a conversation with an angel is like a switch that changes the course of events.

Somewhat of a shocking or an ethereal expectation has been created in man's mind about a possible encounter with the divine or with an angel. This unrealistic expectation makes us miss the encounters that God has planned with life's routine or the ordinary daily affairs of life.

> He comes to our boring days. He refuses to live in the sacred box that we would make for him. He may, of course, be found by those who seek him in special buildings where majestic architecture, painstakingly and lovingly crafted centuries ago, still prophesies his presence in stone. But we mustn't lock him up in those places, lest we shut him out of our ordinary days spent in more mundane places. This Lord of ours has a habit of showing up with surprising news in unusual locations, to the people we would least expect.[98]

Each of us must keep our spiritual antenna tuned in order to anticipate His intervention within the rhythm of modern life. The apostle Paul prayed for the believers in Ephesus so that "the eyes of your heart may be enlightened"[99] in order for them to understand more dimensions of the way in which He works and acts.

After the conversation during which Gideon presented his questions regarding his country's situation, the angel replied:

> "I understood your pain, your dream and the wish to see

your country freed from so much terror and to live a normal life. I have only one message for you: Go with this power that you have and fulfill your dream. Free your country from the hands of the enemy. Am I not sending you?[100]

Go with this power that you have and fulfill your dream. Free your country from the hands of the Enemy. Am not I sending you?

The angel's statement was too shocking for Gideon to accept immediately. What made him doubt this statement was his present state or the context in which he found himself. However, what the angel was stating and the reality Gideon saw with his own eyes in the winepress of despair were diametrically opposed.

We often expect that God will somehow fulfill our dream, prayer or wish, and He often uses this method to put the power in us to fulfill that dream. His power was placed in Gideon exactly like the precious works of art were placed deep underground, with access blocked by multiple layers.

Did you think that you also have the power to fulfill your dream or the calling you have in your heart, but this power is blocked from manifesting?

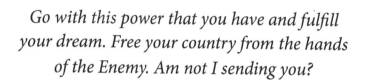

You will meet heavenly messengers that don't have wings like angels, but the conversation with these people will be like a switch that will change the course of events in your life.

Layers of Rubble

The ensuing conversation between Gideon and the angel reveals some of the layers of rubble that cover the treasure of power. These layers and many others that are unidentifiable at a mere glance are the primary factors in the lives of many people that make them ineffective in fulfilling their dream or calling.

Gideon said to him, "Me, my master? How and with what could I ever save Israel?"[101]

Material Possessions

The first obstacle that Gideon considered was material in nature. Many people today also hold this same preconceived notion that only people with money or material possessions can make their dreams a reality. Gideon felt the accomplishment of his dream or calling required having material resources; otherwise, he saw no way to succeed.

He stated, "With what can I save Israel? I look at my circumstances, I look at what I have, and when I look at the resources needed to carry out such a plan, I figure that it is impossible."

Philip considered the problem from the point of view of what the disciples had in their account—✗200 denarii. However, that money obviously could not solve the problem.

By this time in his service with the Savior, Philip had witnessed multiple wonders and miraculous healings that Jesus had performed. In spite of what he had witnessed, Philip was blind to the obvious solution for this problem. The only resolution he saw to feeding hungry people was based on what the disciples had in their account—not on God's miraculous power. He could not connect the information he had about Jesus's power and the situation at hand.

This issue still arises as many people look for answers in life. When they look at their problem and the resources they possess and see the disparity between the two, they feel powerless and depressed. They do not connect the situation they have with God's power.

Another disciple brought a young boy whose lunch contained five loaves and two fishes. Jesus multiplied the boy's lunch, and the myriad of people were fed.

This test for Philip taught him a decidedly valuable lesson that would continue to echo even in our present days. Moments of crisis are situations when His power can manifest. He can solve any problem. He can fulfill any dream or impossible situation even if man has no material ability to resolve it. Man's role is to bring what little he has, entrust that little to His care, and pray that He may multiply and work as He did in these cases.

Had the crowd been sent home hungry, the disciples would

have missed out on experiencing a miracle. They would also have missed out on being utilized in that miracle.

This perspective of situations or dreams that can only be resolved by your means or your loved ones' material assets limit God's manifestation and working. He can do abundantly more than we can imagine because He has all power to resolve every situation in a way only He knows how. What often prevents His working on our behalf are the limitations that we place on Him or wanting the solutions we desire. Faith can manifest wonderfully in times of crises or in the case of unfulfilled dreams.

Influence

Another preconceived notion people hold is the sphere of influence. Gideon said to the angel, *"My family is poor in Manasseh, and I am the least in my father's house."*[105]

This statement underlines the concept that poor families cannot accomplish much. Wealth is associated with influence. If you belong to an affluent family with a high social status, you undoubtedly know what it means to use perks in society. Because of this influence in many avenues of life, you can become successful. If your family is not influentially well-positioned in society, then the dream cannot really be realized. This preconceived notion is the layer of rubble that often covers the accomplishment of dreams or the fulfillment of a calling. This preconceived notion wants to attribute victory and accomplishments to influence rather than to the power that comes from God.

When I was attending seminary in preparation for a ministry, I experienced some incredibly beautiful moments. At the end of my studies, when the time came for me to focus toward a ministry, I was placed in a difficult dilemma that affected me for a long time. Most of my colleagues had parents who were fairly well-rooted in society, others in different ministries. One associate's father was a mission director at a large organization. Another's father was a nationally renowned pastor. Other parents owned prosperous businesses and enjoyed relationships in different domains. For their children, the road before them apparently had already been set. On the other hand, my father had died from cancer when I was 12 years old. In the 90s, we were left on our own.

When I would look at my seminar colleagues and myself and compare our prospects they had before them, fear overtook me. I felt like Gideon, a man with dreams but no chance. Have you ever been down that road where it feels like every avenue is closed for you?

Those are difficult moments when you can let God work and develop His plan in your life, without placing any restrictions, conditions, or boundaries on Him. My prayer during that time was: "God, I declare You to be my Father; do with me as You have planned."

After years and years and looking back at life's zigzags, I can say that God has changed all of the setbacks in my favor. God has demonstrated to me that choosing Him as my Father means He will prepare everything at the right time. *"Father of the fatherless and protector of widows is God in his holy habitation."*[106]

Skill

Another preconceived notion that I have often seen hold people back is skill. Gideon said, "Look, my family is the poorest in Manasseh, and *"I am the youngest in my father's house."*[107]

When you are small or when you see yourself as small, you feel you need help. Those around you are the titans who make the law. Thus, if you are big and tough and you have skills designed to amaze and impose, you can accomplish your dream. If you shine like a star in the night sky, everyone will see you, enabling you to accomplish your dream. On the other hand, if you are the lowest on the social scale, living in a dark tunnel of darkness, you will not find success. This preconceived notion of having to possess skills attributes accomplishing dreams and callings to capability and talents.

Always remember that God does not leave His accomplishments to skill so that He alone receives the glory. He still chooses to do amazing works through people who have nothing about which to vaunt themselves. All the glory belongs to Him!

Wounds

Another obstacle holding many people back stems from wounds of the past. Painful events create a strong emotional connection that causes many to relive that pain through their mind's screen. When they see the string of events again, the questions begin flowing like a rushing river:

* What if it did not happen?

* What if we had approached the situation differently?

* What if we had not gone there?

* What if those words hadn't been spoken?

What if and what if... The wounds make many people into prisoners of their past. Instead of looking at life with hope in the present and future, they spend life with their mind's gaze directed backward toward the painful past. Tied inexorably to what happened to them, they are unable to move forward. They drive the car of life while permanently looking in the rearview mirror. Driving and moving forward is difficult when looking back.

People who continually relive the past are not noticeably concerned with the plans that God has for their lives; rather, their energy is spent reliving past drama and being consoled. For this category of hurt people, the wound is more mentally present than His plan. They need healing in order to be able to overcome past events and begin to use their abilities at a higher level.

Analyze all of the episodes that your mind plays and re-plays and identify those that are tied to past wounds. Pray that God might release you from the difficult past so that you may begin focusing on the new plans that He has for your life.

*Pray that God might release you
from the difficult past so that you may begin focusing
on the new plans that He has for your life.*

Traditionalism

Another layer of rubble that covers the treasure of power, calling and talent in many people's lives is rigid traditionalism.

In ancient times, people devised a way to store and keep wine by using the prepared skin of an animal. At first, the wineskin was flexible, but given time, the skin would become rigid and almost petrified. For an old wine, the wineskin worked well. However, no experienced vintner in Bible times would ever add new wine to an old wineskin. Why? Refilling brittle old wineskins with fresh wine would cause them to burst—like patching an old garment with a new piece of cloth would cause a greater fragility in the fabric. Jesus explained this parable to His disciples, saying, *"And no one pours new wine into old wineskins. Otherwise, the wine will burst the skins, and both the wine and the wineskins will be ruined. No, they pour new wine into new wineskins."*[108]

Religious traditionalism is like an old petrified wineskin. Desiring a new movement of the Holy Spirit will likely end with breaking the old wineskin. Traditionalism means rigidity, believing that the experience of the past is more important and takes precedence over the new.

A new divine discovery that has a fresh and strong fermentation most often comes into conflict with the rules of traditionalism. Many people who have been guided by the Holy Spirit to do something for His kingdom in a new way were hurt by traditional people's ways of thinking.

Traditionalism and experience are the biggest enemies of the Holy Spirit's movement. Why? When God wants to start a new work or redirect a work in another way, traditional people will usually challenge or debate the idea, saying, "Something like that has never been done. The boundaries in which God works are well delineated."

Traditionalism and experience
are the biggest enemies
of the Holy Spirit's innovative movement.

More than likely, you too have observed different layers of rubble covering the treasure of power: incapability, comparison, prisoners of words, inferiority complexes, the mortar of dependence, and prisoners of emotions eating at them. Perhaps you have noticed even more layers than I have described. I want to get more personal and ask you to honestly answer a question. What is the rubble layer that covers and inhibits the treasure of strength in your life to show? What layers have settled over the talents and skills in your life? What stops you from spreading your wings, using your charisma, and flying toward the dream or calling that you have?

Change the Focus

The angel who was, in fact, the Lord, turned Gideon's attention away from what he didn't have and the qualities that he did not possess to God's view of him. The angel changed the "tape" that was playing negative information in his mind, bringing him a new perspective.

> *When the angel of the LORD appeared to Gideon, he said, "The LORD is with you, mighty warrior." The LORD turned to him and said, "Go in the strength you have and save Israel out of Midian's hand. Am I not sending you?"*[109]

No one would have described the young farmer as a *mighty warrior*; however, God's point of view was completely opposite of the reality that he lived and felt. God saw him differently than he saw himself—just like He sees you differently than you see yourself. Most of the time, the heaviness or discouragement that you experience in your circumstances distorts your image of yourself. The image you see is in direct contrast with the way that God sees you.

In her book, *Gideon: Your Weakness. God's Strength*, Priscilla Shirer stated the following:

> Yahweh's perspective on us is often so unbelievable, so foreign to our own belief system and conduct that it can be like a bolt of lightning striking our desensitized

souls. It jolts us away from the misplaced shadows of our experience into the truth of God's reality.[110]

What throws many people into a state of hopelessness and sorrow is that interior voice or the mind's tape that plays their setbacks, their depressing circumstances, the wounds of the past, and a day-by-day account of a somber-looking future. When you allow your mind and your interior voice to repetitiously show the same negative tape, you solicit a state of deep sorrow over your life. The ideas that you feed your mind greatly affect the way you feel and what will happen in your life. The ideas that you feed the placenta of your mind will give birth to those ideas in the material world.

But he said to me, "My grace is sufficient for you, for my power is made perfect in weakness." Therefore I will boast all the more gladly about my weaknesses, so that Christ's power may rest on me (2 Corinthians 12:9 NIV).

Focusing on the disadvantages, weaknesses, and layers of rubble cause them to become all the more pressing and even painful when you compare yourself to others. The Great Artist left them there for a specific purpose; He wants to work through them. The power put into your life needs to become brighter than the pressure of setbacks.

The apostle Paul says that power manifests itself despite our weaknesses: *"For when I am weak, then I am strong."*[111] The attention is shifted from our disadvantages to the treasure of life that offers us freedom from those setbacks, making us available to Him and helping us grow spiritually.

I believe that many a person's problems arise because of focusing on what is lacking and setbacks—not on the power that becomes whole during weakness. On what do you focus?

The power put into your life needs
to become brighter than the pressure of setbacks.

Strength and Weakness

The apostle Paul highlights this law of power and weakness: *"But we have this treasure in jars of clay to show that this all-surpassing power is from God and not from us."*[112]

Life is similar to a fragile ceramic vessel that possesses weaknesses. These disadvantages of the vessel (a human being) may cause a great deal of sorrow, but they must be viewed from a different perspective.

A person's multiple inadequacies, weaknesses and setbacks prevent him from boasting about accomplishing big victories through his own power. That person must recognize that the victory has been accomplished through the power that God put in that vessel. For this reason, *"God chose what is foolish in the world to shame the wise; God chose what is weak in the world to shame the strong."*[113] He chooses people who recognize the source of their victory.

God places an outstanding amount of power in your earthly vessel, and despite your weaknesses and worthlessness, His power will shine brighter. The more you allow the "vessel" to be crushed before Him, the more His power will be set free to manifest itself more intensely. God chose Gideon, who saw himself as weak and inadequate for such a project of freeing the people from under foreign domination. Thus, Gideon experienced a great victory, but he had nothing about which to brag because all of the glory was attributed to God.

I have seen many talented people to whom God does not give resounding victories because they attribute the glory to themselves or brag about what they have accomplished. Hudson Taylor, the great missionary pioneer, once said, "All of God's giants have been weak men who did great things for God because they reckoned on His being with them."[114]

His power manifests itself despite the weakness of the vessel. The more you allow the "vessel" to be crushed before Him, the more His power will be set free to show through the cracks.

A Very Important Place

"Then the angel of the LORD reached out the tip of the staff that was in his hand and touched the meat and the unleavened cakes. And fire sprang up from the rock and consumed the meat and the unleavened cakes. And the angel of the LORD vanished from his sight."[115]

The conversation with "that man" was surprising, but what was shocking was the moment when Gideon brought him some food. After putting the food on the stone, He touched it with the top of his staff and, a fire emerged from the stone, devouring the offering. Then "that man" with the staff was suddenly gone. At that moment, Gideon realized that he had stood face-to-face with "the angel of the Lord."

In that very place, Gideon was convinced that His words would be fulfilled. The burned stone and probably the hole created in the stone by the power of that fire would become the place where he would return in his moments of doubt. To this place he would return when life became difficult and everything seemed contrary to what had been promised to him; he would likely touch that burned spot and the resulting hole to receive courage anew.

To have such a place to go and revisit is valuable like gold; there is where He told you or you were convinced that you must perform a certain work for God. The burnt stone is the sign or symbol that recalibrates you in the work you must do when perhaps circumstances or people are seemingly against you.

When you receive a divine message, record that event or place in your soul's geography as a place that you will have to revisit often.

Less Is More

The Lord said to Gideon, "You have too many warriors with you...."[116]

When Gideon blew the horn, blasting the call to war, thirty-two thousand people gathered. For the farmer Gideon, the presence of that abundance of people was like an incredible spectacle unfolding before his eyes. However, comparing Israel's numbers to the other army numbering one hundred and thirty-five thousand—four times more troops—Gideon probably became dizzy. The contrast in the comparison seemed overwhelming.

God's first requirement for Gideon's army was for the *fearful* to go home. Gideon could not believe his eyes when he saw 22,000 people break ranks and leave. I can only begin to imagine the farmer's heartbroken visage as he stared at the many soldiers leaving who could have helped bring the victory to their nation. Surely, they could have helped or done something for the desperate situation in which the people were all sinking together. Nonetheless, at Gideon's "exception clause," they turned their backs and left. The drastic difference between the size of the two armies rapidly increased before his eyes.

God knew why He asked Gideon to make that announcement. Fear spreads quickly in groups of people. This contagious emotion spreads from one man to another in a startling way. God knew having a small army of brave people was better than having a large one paralyzed by fear. This principle was established in the Hebrews' law of war: *"Is there any man who is fearful and fainthearted? Let him go back to his house, lest he make the heart of his fellows melt like his own."*[117]

In his book, Gideon: Power from Weakness, Jeff Lucas says the following:

Any military tactician will confirm that good morale is vitally important for any army. Whatever their strategic skills and technical proficiency, an army with a broken heart is destined to lose. Fear and negativity are so contagious; therefore, it was important to make sure that only those with a positive attitude remained to fight, lest the battle be lost before it began.[118]

Attitude can be a weapon in the hands of God or in the hands of the Devil. I've observed many people who are not the most capable, but through their good attitudes, they managed to accomplish great things in His kingdom as well as in society. On the other hand, I also observed people who were capable but who were either fearful or had a negative attitude. They were unable to become useful instruments in the hands of God, and their less-than-stellar attitudes caused many others around them to distance themselves.

When I planted the church where I am currently the lead pastor, I had people around me who believed in me and believe in this ministry. They were and are a genuine support. But I have also met friends who refused to be supportive because they feared the work would not flourish or come to fruition. Some others who were a true support had to move to another part of the country with their service. I learned then that you cannot put your hopes in people; rather, you must rely most on the One who gave you the work. If it's God will, then it's God's bill. Each of us will have moments when people will disappoint us, and some will turn their backs on us. Do not forget that He always has people ready to support you in the work that you do or the challenges you go through.

If it's God's will, then it's God's bill.

The LORD said to Gideon, "You have too many warriors with you. If I let all of you fight the Midianites, the Israelites will boast to me that they saved themselves by their own strength."[119]

God said to Gideon, "The 10,000 brave soldiers remaining are too many!"

Gideon replied, "Are there really too many?!"

"Yes, too many. Take them where they can drink water, and I will test them to determine who will go home and who will go with you."

"Ohhhh, God...."

I feel relatively sure Gideon's mind must have been spinning in desperation as he considered how few soldiers the Israelite army compared to the Midianite army.

God then told Gideon to separate all those who knelt to drink water directly from the stream from those who cupped the water in their hands to drink. God instructed him to send home those who did not cup the water in their hands.

The farmer was now left with only 300 warriors. The ratio between the two armies had now increased from 4 to 1 to 450-

to-1 odds. The foreign armies numbered 135,000 people, while Gideon's army consisted of a grand total of 300 people.

I personally do not like these types of conversations or strategies. They disturb the smooth march awaiting us and create deep emotions of doubt. But God's plan is far more important than my plan or yours, for that matter. Following God's plan is more important than my nervousness or what I think is right.

Many leaders would have been taken aback when faced with such a plan and would have considered going into battle suicidal because the odds of winning were totally illogical. Meeting the enemy in battle would be a lost cause.

God wanted to bring Gideon and the children of Israel to the point of total dependence in Him. I have also noticed that many people are afraid of failure because their reputation is important. But God wants to work through the people who consider obeying His voice more important than their reputation or what others might say.

You must reach that point where you have developed such a close relationship with Him that whatever He tells you to do, even when His leading is contrary to appearances or is a certain path to failure, following Him is far more important than your reputation or how you see the situation. Trust me, God sees far beyond what you can see.

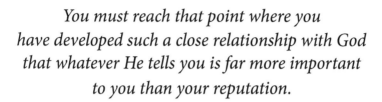

*You must reach that point where you
have developed such a close relationship with God
that whatever He tells you is far more important
to you than your reputation.*

Gideon's army was stripped of any power, so that their victory would totally depend on God. The weakness in His strategy gave the impression of failure, but He did not want to give the victory to some people who would brag on their accomplishments. The disadvantages created a state of dependency on Him and cultivated humility. Once again Gideon saw himself in a position of complete weakness as he contemplated his meager army and a possible strategy to win the battle. However, the treasure of power that God put in him was ready to show. When the chances of victory were impossible, the necessary space was created for God to do His work.

Likewise, the apostle Paul also realized that his weaknesses were the ideal arena for God to do His work. Gideon's army would go to war with a secret weapon: they depended on the Almighty Yahweh.

Divine Strategy

"When the three hundred trumpets sounded, the Lord caused the men throughout the camp to turn on each other with their swords...."[120]

Gideon divided the 300 men into three groups and surrounded the enemy troops. Once the three groups were in place, they blew their trumpets, and broke the pitchers holding the lamps they had brought. The unexpected noise in the middle of the night caused the sleeping soldiers to fight each other instead of the attacking force. The animals were probably frightened and disoriented by the noise and began seeking a way of escape, running around the camp. No doubt, the screams of the wounded and dying amplified the terror in the military camp.

I like the phrase *"the LORD caused...."* God's strategy far surpassed human ability and brought victory. That battle, which has remained memorable to the Hebrew culture, teaches us a valuable lesson: God's power and plan are better than human power and ability. His idea is better than a thousand impressive ideas that will ultimately lead to failure. In life, I prefer to have a single divinely inspired idea, perhaps considered mad by some, that will bring me victory, rather than many impressive but unsuccessful plans.

God's power and plan are better than human power and ability. His idea is better than a thousand impressive ideas that will lead to failure.

Sometimes, after God manifests His power in certain people's lives, He changes some disadvantages, which is exactly what happened in Gideon's life. From starting off as the young farmer who had an insignificant family, he became the most influential leader of that time. A poor man without many skills, he became fairly wealthy and prosperous.

The apostle Paul is a contrasting example because he prayed to God to remove his thorn, a weakness in his body. God chose not to remove that thorn; rather, He gave His servant an even greater grace and utilized him in a powerful way.

Let the treasure of divine power manifest in your life despite weaknesses and setbacks you might have, and you will be blessed. More importantly, God will be glorified.

Reflection Group Questions

1. What are the layers or obstacles you have noticed in your life or in the lives of loved ones that block the God-given talents, skills and spiritual gifts from manifesting?

2. In what way do preconceived notions and lack of faith limit the manifestation of God's power? Use Matthew 13:58 as the foundational text to answer this question.

3. Weaknesses and inabilities can be very difficult, but they can also be the method by which God manifests His power. What did you learn as a result of these experiences?

4. When you look at your soul's geographical map, can you remember divine messages that made a mark and redirected your life's trajectory? Can you describe an event or message that had a strong impact on you?

5. Have you experienced moments when things seemed impossible in life when God worked with very little or through a small number of people but accomplished a lot? Explain what happened and what you learned as a result.

CHAPTER SIX

Memories in the Display Case

"Whoever survives a test, whatever it may be, must tell the story. It is their duty."   – Elie Wiesel

"We will use these stones to build a memorial. In the future your children will ask you, 'What do these stones mean?'

Then you can tell them, 'They remind us that the Jordan River stopped flowing when the Ark of the LORD's Covenant went across.' These stones will stand as a memorial among the people of Israel forever."

                                                      – Joshua 4:6-7 (NLT)

DURING THE LAST few weeks before my wife, Oana, was due to give birth, every call from her was extremely important. The first birth is an unknown road, and the emotions and expectations are always high. About two weeks before the due date, she called and said, "I think it's time for me to go to the hospital. There are some signs, but I am not certain."

"Go to the hospital quickly to see what's going on," I urged. "I'll see you there."

During the consult, the hospital staff said that she would be giving birth soon. Her labor was long and arduous, lasting 29 hours. Finally, at 11:00 at night, I joyfully held our son, Edison William, in my arms.

The doctor said, "I have delivered babies who had the umbilical cord wrapped around their necks three times who were high risk for choking to death. This is the first time in my life when I have delivered a baby with the umbilical cord wrapped around his neck four times."

Hearing those words, I realized that his early arrival by two weeks had been divinely orchestrated. We had prayed for a healthy baby, and the good Lord truly made it so that the baby would be healthy.

After seven and a half years of marriage, I was a dad. Holding Edison in my arms, I felt that my soul was fulfilled. I was receiving congratulatory messages from all over. Oana, as a young mom, was also feeling on top of the world.

However, during the 29 hours of labor, something else had happened that no one had known about. All three of us were in a hospital room when Oana suddenly began to feel some pain and an unbearable internal pressure. At 1:00 a.m., she began to bleed relentlessly. The nurses thought she was experiencing normal postnatal bleeding and tried to assure us that everything would be fine. Seeing her extreme pain, I realized that all was not right. After 45 minutes, she began bleeding profusely again, so much so that the sheets were filled with blood. The nurses changed the blood-soaked linens twice and even weighed them to estimate how much blood had been lost. Realizing that something was indeed wrong, they decided to notify the on-call doctor.

When the doctor checked her status, Oana had a rush of blood that literally burst onto the doctor's arm, soaking her sleeve to shoulder. The doctor immediately realized that Oana was suffering from severe internal hemorrhaging. During the birthing process, a blood vessel had burst within her body.

Before my eyes, I was seeing my darling wife's beautiful color begin to change like a flower that has been without water for a long time. The massive blood loss caused her to lapse into unconsciousness. From the height of joy, I plummeted into the valley of despair.

The medical personnel rushed to move her bed to another room. Additional doctors and nurses came and hovered around her like a swarm of ants, giving her blood, one vial after another. In total, Oana received nearly three liters of life-giving blood.

The issue the doctors combated was that the blood coming in intravenously was flowing out internally through the ruptured blood vessel. I was instructed to stay calm because the hospital had adequate blood supplies.

How calm can I be when my wife is in such a fragile condition?

After conferring, the doctors decided to transport her to

surgery to find the source of the bleeding. Of course, I was not allowed to go in with her. Before she was rushed into surgery, I was instructed, "Say goodbye to her." My eyes opened wide at the command, and I was perplexed beyond belief.

From the tone those two doctors used, my understanding was: *we don't know what is going to happen beyond these doors, and we don't think it will go well.*

I thought I was going to pass out. My soul was struggling within me. It was now 2:45 a.m., and I had no idea what to do. I was left alone as the doors to surgery closed before me. I felt so powerless; the waiting and wondering was like torture. Alone in the hospital hallway, I cried uncontrollably. Edison was in another room. At that moment, I prayed to God to give her life, that was all—life.

"Lord God, that's all I pray, give her life!"

I picked up the phone, and through my tears on that Saturday night, I posted on social media for all friends who were awake to pray **urgently** for my wife, who was in critical condition. The message spread quickly, and I know that many friends and acquaintances prayed for her.

The doctors decided not to operate as surgically finding the source of the bleed could prove impossible. Instead, they urgently called in a team of specialists who could identify the location of the bleed using special equipment and a fluorescent serum inserted into the vein.

I stood in the hospital hallway, desperately hanging on to every hope, praying for her healing and for God to lead the team administering the fluorescent serum to find a solution.

After almost an hour and a half, the medical team came out and one of the doctors said, "We are sorry, but we did not find the location of the bleeding."

I was left speechless. At that moment, my whole inner world shook to its core. I felt almost as though the sky had fallen on me. I was at the end of my wits.

It was now Sunday morning.

Many of our pastor friends who had seen my post reached out to their church families, letting them know about our situation. The church families began praying for Oana and our situation. The doctors kept Oana under very close observation during those hours, but they still did not know what to do.

That morning, I received a call from a pastor in Europe who said, "Adrian, today our whole congregation prayed for your situation. I want to tell you that someone from our congregation in the audience had a vision—a message from God—about your situation. The man said that he saw *a white hand* operating on your wife. I don't know her exact medical condition, but I called to give you the message."

I was in shock. I hung up and, after a few hours, Oana was transferred to the room where I was waiting. The doctor explained, "We know where the rupture occurred, but we haven't found the exact location of the bleeding. The good news is that *somehow* the bleeding has stopped."

Although the doctors had done the best they could do humanly speaking, they were unable to stop the bleeding. For us, a miracle had stopped the bleeding. I can still see *the white hand* that operated on her through the eyes of my faith.

After a few more days of monitoring and tests, my wife was discharged, and we were able to pack up and go home. As we were packing our belongings, I found Oana's white sock that she had been wearing when she was lying in the pool of blood on the sheets. The sock was primarily stained with blood, and my first instinct was to discard it and forget about what had happened. Something inside me said, "Don't throw it out."

In those moments, I remembered the Hebrew people who stood before the impossible—the River Jordan that they had to cross to reach the Promised Land. Their leader, Joshua, said, "When the river miraculously stops and you cross on dry land, take a stone from the middle of it, and build a monument to remind you of the experience."

Later on, Joshua told them, "When your children [or grand-children] ask you, 'What do these stones mean?'[121] you tell them that they symbolize God's intervention in the impossible—the critical situation that you went through. Thus, teach them about His power and what He has done for you."

Each experience in which we see His marks, we have a duty to take a souvenir to remind us of what He has done for us. Therefore, I kept the bloody sock—not to remember the unfortunate event nor the desperation that I went through, but to remember the white hand—the hand of Jehovah Rapha.[122] I took it home and put it in the display case of memories of the soul, together with other souvenirs that stood as a testimony to my walk with God. The remembrance stones from the display case of the soul represent the divine interventions on the soul's geographical map.

I remember that the Colombian writer Gabriel García Márquez described the human need to remember in such beautiful words: "What matters in life is not what happens to you but what you remember and how you remember it."[123]

The remembrance stones from the display case of the soul represent the divine interventions on the soul's geographical map.

I believe that we each have different pictures, souvenirs or memories from life's beautiful moments—photos with family or friends, wedding photos, trophies earned, pictures of pets we have loved, and many other precious memories that remind us of the beautiful moments we have lived. Life is practically made of such memories.

However, each of us has a display glass of spiritual memories in which we place and keep souvenirs that remind us of His interventions. This display case grows as we collect different souvenirs from our experiences that become part of our memories and symbols. If you look at the map of your soul, you will notice failures and critical situations turned into victories because of God's miraculous interventions, healings, and doors opened especially for you. You can take a little something from each of these to remind you of His power and faithfulness.

I like how Ann Voskamp set this reality before us: "We, the

people with chronic soul amnesia, are called to be the remembering people."[124]

These souvenirs from the midst of suffering or miracles are a source of faith and trust for future difficult moments in life or testimonies for those who go through hard times. This display case of memories is a sacred place. It is the most fertile ground for faith to grow because it reminds you of what God has done in the past and gives you hope during life's crises.

The display case of memories is a sacred place.
It is the most fertile ground for faith to grow
because it reminds you what God has done
in the past and gives you hope during life's crises.

The Bible sprinkles the concept of remembering in the lives of many people. At 25 years of age, Hezekiah ascended to the throne of Judah's land. He was a young man full of energy and faith who stood out through many good acts. His accomplishments made him a beloved and prized king of the people and, from all points of view, he was at the top of the pyramid. Life was beautiful for him; however, once he reached 39 years of age, he became ill. A mass developed in his body, and the germs from the purulence entered his bloodstream. His was a case of septicemia, as some specialists say, and the doctors at that time could not find a cure. The entire kingdom was on alert because of the illness, which was worsening day by day;

even neighboring kingdoms spoke about his condition. During those days of illness, the prophet Isaiah visited him with a message from God: *"Put your house in order, because you are going to die; you will not recover"* (2 Kings 20:1).

The prophet's message was like a lightning bolt that shook Hezekiah to his core. The young king's life was like a pendulum oscillating between a life lived at the top of the pyramid to the other extreme—the brink of death. Just as the divine messenger had said, the last pages were soon going to be ripped out of his life's calendar.

I would not want to experience such moments, and I don't think that you would either. As we go through life, we realize how fragile life is. I think we all know people who lived in enviable circumstances with life smiling at them from each direction as they climbed the steps of social ladders, when suddenly, the pendulum stopped, and they began to descend in the other direction.

The lives of many people have been redirected by an abandonment, a divorce, the death of a loved one, a difficult diagnosis, the unexpected loss of work, bankruptcy, separation, cheating, or betrayal. Life sometimes brings moments of oscillating between extremes of happiness and tragedies. Those moments when we go through one state to another are like lightning bolts that light up our reality to the brevity of life and wake us up to the ideals we aspire to fulfill.

When the sheets in our calendar are counted, and we have little left to live, we start to somewhat realize what is truly valuable. During those moments, no one would have wished to stay at work longer to earn more, to have practiced their hobby longer or been someone who they really are not. Those are the moments when we realize how short life is, what the true values are and that we should have spent more time with the loved ones in our lives.

"Teach us to number our days, that we may gain a heart of wisdom" (Psalm 90:12 NIV).

When the sheets in our calendar are counted, and we have little left to live, we somewhat start to realize what is truly valuable.

As young King Hezekiah heard the echo of Isaiah's words, *"You will die; you will no longer live,"*[125] he laid down on his bed facing the wall and began to pray and cry uncontrollably. He cried out to God:

"Remember, LORD, how I have walked before you faithfully and with wholehearted devotion and have done what is good in your eyes."[126]

In response, God looked down from the high heavens at the young king, saw his tears, heard his prayer and promptly answered him. He sent Isaiah back to the royal chamber with another message:

"I have heard your prayer and seen your tears; I will heal you. I will add fifteen years to your life."[127]

Isaiah's medication of choice was surprising. He instructed the king's caregivers to place a fig tart on the swelling, and in three days he would be healed.

When experiencing spiritual or physical pain, there is an impression of loneliness in suffering, and that no one understands what the sick person is going through. I would like to get more personal and remind you that as God saw into the young king's room, He also sees into your life as well. He sees our suffering, the tears we shed that sometimes no one else sees, and He is not indifferent to our situation. The Bible says that God takes each of our tears and puts it into His bottle, then dries our cheeks.[128]

We have fragmented life into different compartments: work, family, fun, vacations, church, etc. Our finite minds have created an idea of what is sacred and what is profane, meaning God is in His space at church, we visit Him on Sundays, then we leave Him in His home and come back next time to see Him. But our God goes beyond our compartments and limits we put on Him, and He gets to the bed of our suffering or to the car where we cry while we drive or to the kitchen where we serve dinner.

He is everywhere, and He cares about us! He cares about you!

God goes beyond the limits that we have place on Him and reaches the bed of our suffering. He is everywhere, and He cares about us! He cares about you.

Perhaps the situation that you are going through right now is complicated and, humanly speaking, you do not see any solution to resolve it, just as King Hezekiah felt hearing that the doctors had no solution. I want to remind you that God is beyond medicine, human resources, and man's capabilities. Just as God gave the young king a healing solution beyond the understanding of medicine at the time, He can also give you a solution to your problem and your pain that is beyond your ability to understand. He has incredible prescriptions for your situation. Whatever your problem may be, whether financial, relational, emotional, medical, and perhaps even at work or of any other nature, don't forget that God has solutions you have not even considered. Pray to Him, put your problem before Him, and just as He did with the young king, He will answer you.

"Do not be anxious about anything, but in every situation, by prayer and petition, with thanksgiving, present your requests to God. And the peace of God, which transcends all understanding, will guard your hearts and your minds in Christ Jesus."[129]

The Purpose of the Remembrance Stones

After the young king recovered, he composed a song expressing how short life is while God, in His kindness, had prolonged the thread of his life. The song became known by all the people and became a hymn in Hebrew culture—like a remembrance stone underlining divine intervention after prayer.

Like a shepherd's tent my house has been pulled down and taken from me.

Like a weaver I have rolled up my life, and he has cut me off from the loom; day and night you made an end of me.

I cried like a swift or thrush, I moaned like a mourning dove.

My eyes grew weak as I looked to the heavens. I am being threatened; Lord, come to my aid!"

But what can I say?

He has spoken to me, and he himself has done this.

I will walk humbly all my years because of this anguish of my soul.

Lord, by such things people live; and my spirit finds life in them too.

You restored me to health and let me live![130]

The first purpose of the souvenirs in the soul's display case of memories is to *remember divine interventions*. Many people from the pages of the Bible had different experiences that marked their lives and the different souvenirs they gathered reminded them of divine intervention.

After David fought the lion and the bear, he likely brought home the lion's skin and the bear's fur because they would serve as valuable coverings, but at the same time, they would remind him of past victories. Thus, his confidence began to grow. When he went to fight Goliath, he told Saul that he was not afraid of the giant because he already had a history of victories; the lion's skin and bear's fur were his testimony. After he had defeated the giant, he took the weapons from him and brought them to his tent. David was a collector of souvenirs.

In your life as well, many future battles will be won on the shoulders of past victories.

Gideon had a special place he liked to visit. When he brought his offering, God touched it and a strong flame ignited from the stone and burned it, turning the food into coal.[131] That burnt, blackened stone, which probably had an indentation in it from the flame, was the place where Gideon was "burned" into the ministry. In his moments of doubt, he would revisit this place for reassurance about the work he had to do. The burnt stone was an important place that became part of his display case of memories.

The place where you were called to ministry will remain in your soul as a place where you will find reassurance and strength to keep moving forward.

Rahab, the prostitute, hung a red rope outside her window to remind the Hebrews spies of their promise to save her and her family during the battle. Once Rahab was saved, I can imagine that she kept that red rope for the rest of her life as it was the rope of salvation. *What is the souvenir that reminds you of the story of your salvation?*

Habakkuk had a place where he would pray. To all of his questions and worries,

The LORD answered me and said, "Record the vision and inscribe it on tablets, That the one who reads it may run. For the vision is yet for the appointed time; It hastens to-

ward the goal and it will not fail. Though it tarries, wait for it; For it will certainly come, it will not delay."[132]

I can imagine Habakkuk's holding the tablets with the divine message close to his chest, reading them often and remembering the promise made to him. After the promise was fulfilled, he probably kept the tablets in a safe place.

Keep the messages you received from Him in a sacred journal. The song that the young King Hezekiah composed remained a personal and national hymn that reminded Hebrews of the miraculous healing and of how God had extended the thread of life.

What souvenir did you bring from the time of illness that you went through?

The list of biblical examples is extensive, but the underlying message is the same—the need to develop a display case of the soul with different objects, places, messages or other elements that would bear the marks of divine intervention in the story of our life. In reality, these objects themselves are not necessarily valuable, but they have great value because they hold the memory of an experience, a declaration or an important event.

Without the objects, the stories would lack vibrancy; without the stories, the objects would lack significance. Taken together, the images of the objects, the memories they evoke and the stories of their collection take the viewer on a journey where the commonplace is transformed into the remarkable and where the stuff of history is highly personalized.[133]

The second purpose of the souvenirs in the soul's display case of memories is to *lift up those around you.*

> *"I waited patiently for the* LORD *to help me, and he turned to me and heard my cry. He lifted me out of the pit of despair, out of the mud and the mire. He set my feet on solid ground and steadied me as I walked along. He has given me a new song to sing, a hymn of praise to our God.* **Many will see what he has done and be amazed. They will put their trust in the** LORD*"* (Psalm 40:1-3 NLT).

These verses hold within them an exact paradigm for growing others' faith. The paradigm to note is the following:

a) **Prayer**—the call of the person going through a hard time

b) **Divine intervention**—salvation from hardship

c) **Testimony**—the song of praise after divine intervention

d) **The Effect of the experience**—others' faith in God after the situation endured by the person going through hardship.

When those around us hear our testimony, whether through a song, a story, a location or a souvenir attached to a personal story, the effect of the experience will bring encouragement and faith in God. Testimonies are part of the spiritual treasures that must be kept and shown because they are a source of encouragement for those going through difficult times. When you see someone going through a deep valley and you tell them the story of the deep valley that you experienced, perhaps sharing your stone of remembrance that you saved from there will catapult the misfortunate one from the valley of despair into the perimeter of faith.

After Goliath was defeated, David brought the giant's weapons into his tent, but he took Goliath's sword to Nob. The citadel of Nob was a priestly town where the Tabernacle was and where the Hebrews went to pray. Seeing Goliath's sword also reminded them of David's victory in that unequal battle. That image, which was a testimony of victory, developed people's faith that they could also be victorious in disproportionate battles.

A third purpose of the souvenirs in the soul's display case of memories is to *glorify God*.

"Sing to the Lord, *bless his name; tell of his salvation from day to day.*

*Declare his glory among the nations, his **marvelous** **works** among all the peoples!*

For great is the Lord, *and greatly to be praised; he is to be feared above fall gods"* (Psalm 96:2-4 ESV).

Those who have gone through experiences where they saw divine intervention have a duty to proclaim His glory. The remembrance stones are not about us, and we are not the heroes; He alone is the author and performer of miracles. These experiences have a specific purpose of drawing attention to God and glorify Him.

This triple-braided cord, a reminder of divine interventions, lifting up those around and glorifying God, is the golden rope that will keep you standing through life's storms.

The Attack on the Remembrance Stones

The souvenirs or remembrance stones describing divine intervention will always be the Devil's target. He is the sniper hunting them to destroy the viability of the paradigm for growing faith. His evil intent is to destroy them by giving them new meaning or creating a new history for them. He is a specialist in reinterpreting history, misinforming, stealing credit and manufacturing a new story of the past.

What Happened in Young King Hezekiah's life?

Young Hezekiah promised to go through his entire life with piety and to recognize that God is the One who brought him healing. Shortly after that near-death experience, his life returned somewhat to normal. Having heard of his illness and recovery and other miracles that had taken place in the land, the king of Babylon sent some officials to him with a gift. Hezekiah received them well and told them about how he had been on the brink of death and then became well and healthy. He failed to recognize before them that God was the author of the healing.

"However, when ambassadors arrived from Babylon to ask about the remarkable events that had taken place in the land, God withdrew from Hezekiah in order to test him and to see what was really in his heart."[134]

*"But Hezekiah did not respond appropriately to the kindness shown him, and **he became proud**...."*[135]

The king had to testify before the diplomats that his healing and the fact that he was still alive was a miracle performed by God. However, his heart became filled with pride, and he did not point to God but served as the gasoline feeding his pride and ego.

When pride does not recognize that He is the author of the miracle and instead takes the glory of what happened miraculously upon itself, the story of that spiritual experience is reinterpreted. Likewise, the paradigm for growing others' faith in God stops working, and His fame is dulled. Man becomes a thief of glory.

I have often noticed in moments of sorrow when we are out of solutions, we pray and need God to help us. After we receive His help, somehow the story of divine intervention is generalized and forgotten. The reinterpretation makes its way in, pride puts in its point of view, and suddenly, God is no longer the Author. Man becomes the center of what happened as everything develops into "look at what happened and how I solved it." This attitude is part of the attack on the spiritual display case of memories, the purpose of which is to reinterpret and cover up divine fingerprints.

*When God gives you a victory, that experience
is part of the treasure of your faith, and
that very experience will become the Devil's target.*

Napoleon Bonaparte headed toward Russia to conquer it with an army of over 500 thousand soldiers. In June of 1812, the French army entered Russian territory. King Alexander I, the leader of Russia, was young, dissolute, and unprepared for such a confrontation.

Napoleon's fame as a conqueror scared the Russian tsar and, of course, he could foresee what would happen if they were to be conquered. Russian records say that, in his panic, Alexander I entered into the Saint Petersburg Cathedral and, looking up toward heaven, prayed, asking God to intervene and save him. He promised that if divine Providence would watch over him, he would build a cathedral as a monument to remain in the country's memory as testimony.

When the French army undertook the military expedition, they failed to account for the Russian winter, which decimated Napoleon's well-conceived plans. The winter cold that began to settle over Russia was the divine agent through which heaven was answering the tsar's prayer. When Napoleon's armies arrived in Moscow, they expected to find a city full of people to fight, and once defeated, they would acquire the resources they desperately needed. Because the tsar had

ordered the burning of Moscow, Napoleon's troops were unable to obtain the needed supplies. Their lack of preparedness for the frigid winter cold, the lack of resources and the lack of food destroyed the French army. The resulting human loss was tragic.

When Napoleon Bonaparte retreated from Moscow and fled back to France, Tsar Alexander I signed a manifest on December 25, 1812, declaring his intention to build a Christ the Savior Cathedral "to signify our gratitude...for God's Providence, which has saved Russia from imminent ruin."[136]

Of course, historians have spent a great deal of ink explaining in detail what occurred; however, what I wish to highlight is that during those desperate times, Tsar Alexander I asked for the help of Divine Providence, and He protected them. This episode remained written in the archives of history, and he also kept his promise and built a beautiful cathedral in Moscow, a construction project which lasted 40 years. The Christ the Savior Cathedral was a symbol of divine intervention in their favor that keeps the events of that troubled time in the minds and conscience of the people.

A few decades after the cathedral was completed, a new political party arrived on the political stage that instated an atheistic paradigm in all of Russia. This new party aimed to indoctrinate people with atheism through books, newspapers, parades, movies, and, especially by transforming churches and cathedrals into museums of atheism.[137]

In her book, *A Sacred Space Is Never Empty: A History of Soviet Atheism*, the historian Victoria Smolkin stated:

This museumification of religion transformed sacred objects and spaces into sanitized cultural artifacts. They were considered most effective when they occupied religious spaces that had been repurposed for atheist use. Indeed, the most prominent antireligious museums were established on the grounds of some of the country's most important monasteries and churches.[138]

St. Isaac Cathedral in Saint Petersburg, the place where Tsar Alexander I prayed for divine intervention remained in Russia's history as a place of great spiritual weight, but the atheist ideology transformed that cathedral into a museum of atheism and science. Likewise, Christ the Savior Cathedral, a monument that had been destined to remind people of divine intervention and of the soldiers who had fought, was a target of atheism.

On December 5, 1931, by order of Joseph Stalin, the Cathedral of Christ the Savior was dynamited and reduced to rubble in order to build a large modern Soviet center. However, for a long time, that place was only a pool. Another 250 places of worship were turned into museums and educational centers in the name of science and atheism.

From these examples, I wish to highlight that the monuments or remembrance stones, either at the national level or personal level, will be under attack by the Evil One to destroy the process of educating others and to erase from someone's personal history or a people's history the symbols or testimonies of divine intervention. The Devil wants to destroy these educational testimonies of the fact that God works and is active in the history of the world.

The remembrance stones are of great importance to spiritual development. When placed side by side, they help you to rise in faith. If you destroy their meaning or steal their copyrights, you are stealing God's prints from the life of man. The reinterpretation of history has always been the Devil's specialty.

*The monuments or remembrance stones,
either at the national level or pesonal level, will be
under attack by the Evil One to destroy the process
of educating others and to erase from someone's
personal history or a people's history the symbols
or testimonies of divine intervention.*

Managing Spiritual Experiences and Remembrance Stones

Some of the difficult times in life or various wars that I have gone through have often left deep wounds. I have often noticed that even if we have unexpected victories or the situation turns in our favor, we are much more preoccupied with the wounds of the past than with proclaiming present victory. I wonder why the wounds of the past are more vivid and more palpable than proclaiming victory or the remembrance stones? The wounds of the past can be used as a weapon in the hands of the

Devil to steal our joy, and the victories can lose value for this very reason. Each of us is responsible to manage our spiritual experiences and remembrance stones well because they can affect multiple areas of our lives.

The remembrance stones affect the spiritual dimension of the next generations.

Remember the children of Israel preparing to cross Jordan? The monument built with the stones in the Jordan River was destined to be a place of remembrance. The altar of stones was to speak to the Hebrews about the way in which they had miraculously passed through the waters of the Red Sea, the manna that Providence had fed them in the desert, and the waters of the River Jordan that stopped to let them pass to the banks of the Promised Land.

Joshua ordered the people to tell their children what the stones meant. They were responsible to testify and teach them about what had happened since the exodus from Egypt. Likewise, the responsibility of every parent who has gone through "teaching" experiences is to keep the meaning of those remembrance stones alive, offering personalized explanations about the miracles that God performed. However, something tragic happened during the next generation's time.

> *"And all that generation also were gathered to their fathers. And there arose another generation after them who did not know the LORD or the work that he had done for Israel"* (Judges 2:10 ESV).

The following generation did not know about God nor about

His interventions. Something tragic happened between Joshua 4 when the monument was created and Judges 2:10—the spiritual declivity of the next generation. The monument was still standing; however, the meaning behind it—the testimony of the divine interventions—had been abandoned.

One of the great problems of that generation was managing testimony, i.e., the remembrance stones. The effect of this depreciation was transposed to the spiritual fiber of the children, grandchildren, and great-grandchildren. The Hebrew people began to live without a moral compass. Everything was permitted: *"everyone did what was right in his own eyes."*[139] Approximately 410 years of chaos and subjugation followed, a time during which approximately 15 political judges appeared and tried to steer the nation away from the abyss into which it had fallen.

Sometimes we get the impression that talking about what has happened is not so important, or perhaps that others are not interested. But the message is like a seed that, when placed in the ground at the right time, will bear fruit.

The book of Proverbs states: *"Train up a child in the way he should go; even when he is old, he will not depart from it."*[140]

At other times, we allow ourselves to be controlled by worry and fear, or we forget and neglect the past monuments and testimonies. Sometimes other priorities gain importance and take over our thoughts that lead us and that we show; thus, we put aside showing the spiritual testimonies that can educate and prepare the next generation.

If you remember a mountain that you got over only with His help, tell a loved one about that experience.

If you have stood before a Goliath who threatened you with illness or a difficult situation, and you came out victorious, write about that in the diary of memories.

If you have been through a great storm and still were able to reach the shore, tell about that story and point all glory to Him.

If you do not keep the place where you started vividly in your mind, what you went through, and where you surpassed the situation, then you will lose the value of what God gave you. You will begin to believe that it was through your own powers or that what happened is something "normal."

It is our duty to manage our spiritual experiences well because they will influence the next generations.

The remembrance stones affect whether or not we repeat history.

In 1944, the train that young Elie Wiesel, his family and other Jews who had been taken from Sighet, Transylvania, were riding entered through the gates of Auschwitz. Hitler gathered up Jews from various countries in Europe and took them to the Nazi concentration camps.

Elie Wiesel was 15 years old when he arrived there. He was waiting in line to be "assigned" when someone whispered to him, "When they ask you how old you are, tell them you are 18 years old." That information saved him from the cruel experiments that Dr. Joseph Mengele was performing on children and especially on twins. The merciless Dr. Mengele, who was nicknamed the "Angel of Death," pointed to the newcomers in line with his cane and then gestured which direction to go—to the left or to the right. To the right meant to the ovens where they would be burned after being gassed. To the left meant living in the concentration camp.

In his book, *Night,* Wiesel tells how he saw his mother and his sister Tzipora with his own eyes standing before the Angel of Death, who pointed at them with his cane and gestured for them to proceed to the right.

> In a fraction of a second, I could see my mother, my sister, move to the right. Tzipora was holding Mother's hand. I saw them walking farther and farther away; Mother was stroking my sister's blond hair, as if to protect her. And I walked on with my father, with the men. I didn't know that this was the moment in time and the place where I was leaving my mother and Tzipora forever.[141]

Words cannot describe the atrocities that took place in those concentration camps, where millions died in such cruel ways nor the spiritual wounds that constantly bleed of the few who came out alive from those places.

Elie's father passed away a few days before the U.S. Third Army arrived to free them on April 11, 1945. Elie Wiesel was transported to France, along with 1,000 other children who survived the horrors there. Later on, he enrolled in school and, at 19 years of age, he began to work as a journalist writing articles for different newspapers in Israel and in France.

The atrocities experienced, the deaths of his loved ones, the interminable suffering, the images of children and adults being gassed then thrown into the ovens of Auschwitz haunted Wiesel from within. He stated:

> I knew that the role of the survivor was to testify.... I made a vow: not to speak, not to touch upon the essential for at least ten years. Long enough to see clearly. Long enough to learn to listen to the voices crying inside my own. Long enough to regain possession of my memory. Long enough to unite the language of man with the silence of the dead.[142]

A conversation with the famous French writer François Mauriac made him change his point of view about the testimony that he had to give regarding the horrors of Auschwitz through which he had lived. François Mauriac graciously shared,

> "I think that you are wrong. You are wrong not to speak... Listen to the old man that I am: one must speak out—one must *also* speak out." One year later I sent him the manuscript of *Night*, written under the seal of memory and silence.[143]

The duty of the one who survives the test, whatever that test may be, is to bear witness. Certainly, opening the still bloody wounds of the past and putting them on the table before others who might hit you right in that spot can be extremely difficult, but if no one testifies about the horrors that took place, they can be repeated elsewhere.

The philosopher and essayist George Santayana said, "Those who cannot remember the past are condemned to repeat it." The experiences of the past can be positive or painful, but they have a role in educating those who come after. Likewise, our spiritual experiences must be presented to our children and our loved ones so that they may teach them to repeat the good and avoid the wrong.

Alfred Eichmann, one of the masterminds behind the Holocaust, fled to Argentina under a false name once the Jews were freed. He remained there for many years and tried to create a new Nazi movement, *Operation Finale*. A team of spies from the Hebrew Mossad (Institute for Intelligence and Special Operations) heard that Alfred Eichmann was hiding in Argentina. The agents tracked him down, captured him, extradited him to Israel, and later prosecuted him for the atrocities he had committed.

Perhaps that connection was a reason for Elie Wiesel's first book being published in Argentina. Perhaps he desired to educate public opinion on what Nazism and the Holocaust meant so that the movement would not be repeated in their own country.

Those who do not learn from history
are doomed to repeat it.

The remembrance stones affect decisions.

Remembering the critical situations you have experienced or your difficult beginnings has this role of keeping you in a state of piety and appreciation. When you forget where you came from and what God has done for you, you open the door for pride to gain territory in your life. The Evil One can do great harm with the weapon of pride.

After his experiences, King Hezekiah allowed himself to become filled with pride. When the Babylonian officers visited him, the king received them well and started to show off his country's wealth, the weapons he had, where the weapons were located, and the power at his disposal. Simply, he showed them everything. At that time, as is true now, espionage was an essential element of retaining power. The officers took mental notes of everything that they could.

How wise would it be for the President of the United States to show visiting dignitaries from the Middle East or Asia the U.S.'s wealth and weapons, and where they are held? How wise would it be for him to show them the country's power and abilities?

Pride caused Hezekiah to show them the power at his disposal to impress them. He had forgotten that *"Pride goes before destruction, and a haughty spirit before a fall."*[144] Pride leads to the fall of those who mindlessly think they are immune to their weaknesses. Pride is the flower that grows on the grave of humility.

"What did they see in your palace?" Isaiah asked.

"They saw everything," Hezekiah replied. "I showed them everything I own—all my royal treasuries."

Then Isaiah said to Hezekiah, "Listen to this message from the LORD: The time is coming when everything in your palace—all the treasures stored up by your ancestors until now—will be carried off to Babylon. Nothing will be left, says the LORD."[145]

The Babylonian officers, who were spying under the guise of friendship, were actually collecting information about the country's resources, the weapons capabilities, the geographic positioning of the citadel, and any other ascertainable information. The prophet Isaiah confronted the king and told him that he had made a great mistake by showing off his treasures. That decision, which had been fueled by pride, would lead to all of the riches being taken to Babylon in the future.

The Babylonians' strategy matched the Devil's strategy. He comes like a subtle snake under the guise of friendship and then attacks fiercely like a lion. His target is the place of power and abilities, to weaken and to destroy.

Likewise, when the powerful Samson fell prey to the charm and caresses of the prostitute, Delilah, she finally needed to ask only a single question: "Tell me the secret of your great strength and how you can be tied up and subdued."[146]

He opened his heart and told her the secret of his strength. Delilah's strategy was to envelop him in her charms and thereafter cutting off the source of his strength, and she hit him in that very spot. The Babylonians' strategy was to use the guise of friendship, after which their armies invaded the land, mercilessly wreaking havoc and destruction. The Devil's strategy is to invade with the subtlety of the snake, after which he strikes like a lion.

The true Christian's source of strength is his relationship with God—the time spent reading the Bible and in prayer, receiving His guidance and the continual presence of the Holy Spirit. Pride, however, will push many to believe that they are self-sufficient and do not need God or His guidance, but the Devil will attack them right in their source of strength to weaken or disable them. When the Christian receives no divine guidance in making decisions, then pride will push him into making unwise decisions that will likely have repercussions on his children and grandchildren.

> *The time is coming when everything in your palace—all the treasures stored up by your ancestors until now—will be carried off to Babylon. Nothing will be left, says the* LORD. *Some of your very own sons will be taken away into exile. They will become eunuchs who will serve in the palace of Babylon's king.*
>
> *Then Hezekiah said to Isaiah,* **"This message you have given me from the LORD is good."** *For the king was thinking,* **"At least there will be peace and security during my lifetime."**[147]

Hezekiah's pride in trying to impress with what he had and failing to recognize God's steadfastness had repercussions for his descendants. Because of his decisions, Daniel, together with many other young people, were led to slavery to the Babylon.

I was most surprised by the king's words of indifference: *"The word of God that you have told me is good, because there will be peace and quiet during my lifetime."* Hezekiah's philosophy was "as long as it's good for me, no problem." He minimized the importance of family and their future.

A comparison of Hezekiah and Caleb reveals two opposing philosophies about family. At eighty years of age, Caleb asked Joshua to let him conquer a mountain full of giants so that when he died, his children would not live under threat from the enemy nor with an uncertain future. In other words, Caleb did all he could to leave stability, prosperity, blessings and a calm future for his children and future generations. Caleb thought in terms of blessing generations after him; Hezekiah thought in terms of "as long as I'm well..." Future generations can face their own problems.

Your family's future is extremely important. The decisions you make today are like a seed planted in the ground; your children will reap the fruits. Invest in your future and the next generation by making decisions centered on God.

The decisions you make today
are like a seed planted in the ground;
your children will reap the fruits.

I ask you again at the end of this chapter: what are the remembrance stones in your display case of memories? Are you determined to gather more souvenirs? Will you share all He has done for you with your children and those around you to build memories for them? Will you recognize God's intervention in the difficult times in your life? When you look back at your life's story, will you see His fingerprints? If yes, then share these remembrance stones in your display case of memories with someone.

Reflection Group Questions

1. What are some of the souvenirs or remembrance stones that are in your mind's display case reminding you of divine interventions in your life? What do they reveal or symbolize?

2. Tell about an experience in which you applied the paradigm in Psalm 40:1-3. What did you learn? How did it impact your faith?

3. How does the Evil One try to steal people's spiritual experiences and souvenirs?

4. How can you manage your spiritual experiences so that you do not lose their value?

5. How will your spiritual experiences affect your children or the next generation? What can you do so that your children learn from these experiences and continue to grow spiritually?

CHAPTER SEVEN

My Problem and My Solution

"Often man's disappointments are God's appointments, but we can only discover His purpose in them as we respond in faith."   – Derek Prince

"When they came to Marah, they could not drink its water because it was bitter. So the people grumbled against Moses, saying, "What are we to drink?" Then Moses cried out to the LORD, and the LORD showed him a piece of wood. He threw it into the water, and the water became fit to drink...."   – Exodus 15:23-25 (NIV)

I N 1990, THE SITUATION in Vietnam was a painful one. Over 65 percent of the children under the age of five suffered from malnutrition. Seeing their swollen bellies and their flesh so emaciated that every rib showed was horrific. Disease and powerlessness loomed in the air.

The Vietnamese government asked the "Save the Children"

foundation to get involved in this problem and to assist in finding a permanent solution. Save the Children sent Jerry Sternin to help in this project. When Jerry arrived, the Vietnamese Minister of External Affairs met him at the airport, and among other things, shared, "You have six months to demonstrate impact."[148]

Pressed for time and by the situation there, Sternin began to observe customs and collect information. He saw the haunting poverty, the lack of pure drinking water, and the precarious hygiene situation. He also noticed a clear rule that the community had regarding feeding children. The family ate together twice a day and only soft food intended for children. The rice had to be of the best quality.

However, even with the poverty, he also noticed that some poor families had healthy, well-developed children. He was both surprised and curious as to how such healthy children could be reared in poor families when so many were ill. Shortly thereafter, he reached the conclusion that the solution to the people's malnutrition might be right there among them, but somehow remained hidden from their eyes.

He studied those poor families who had healthy children, and he noticed something interesting. Mothers would feed their children the same amount of food, but they would split it into four meals per day (as opposed to the others that fed them only two meals per day) because a child's stomach was unable to process so much food at once. They gave their children a varied diet, putting shrimp, crabs, sweet potato and greens in the children's rice. The children were also encouraged to eat when they were sick in order to get better."[149]

These poor mothers had found the solution to the malnutrition problem because they had gone beyond the common consensus on what and when children should eat.

Sternin understood that the solution had been discovered by a few mothers but had to be implemented into society at large. Therefore, he created a program to teach mothers how to prepare varied meals, when to feed the children, how and when to use soap when preparing food, and also to wash the children. Sternin's success began to spread all over.

> "The program reached 2.2 million Vietnamese people in 265 villages. Our living university has become a national model for teaching villagers to drastically reduce malnutrition in Vietnam," Sternin said.[150]

Life hits all of us with critical situations that throw many of us into a corner of despair, not knowing what to do. The example of the sick children in Vietnam suggests that the solution to the crisis that we are experiencing is frequently hidden within the problem. The answer is present there but hidden from people's eyes due to habit, social etiquette, myths or other factors.

Crisis situations are like a switch meant to redirect our lives or reveal something to us about ourselves or about God. And so, we need to have our minds and our eyes lit up by God in order to see beyond that which is visible—to see in the spiritual dimension—the key to opening the door to resolving the situation.

Thus the prophet Elisha also prayed for his servant: *"O LORD, please open his eyes that he may see."*[151] And the servant then saw beyond what he could see with his human eyes; the solution that was present in the midst of the crisis was revealed to him.

This chapter is an invitation to examine problems from a different perspective—to look beyond what our human eyes view and see His purposes and solutions that come together with the problems.

The solution is often hidden within the problem, but it must be discovered.

From Blessing to Bitterness

The example of the Hebrew people traveling to the Promised Land highlights exactly this aspect of the purpose and solution hidden within the crisis. At both the Red Sea and the Jordan River, the waters split before them in the same way a lumberjack would split a log. As the water rose up like walls, a path was formed across the dry bed between the two walls. What happened was simply incredible!

The approximately three million former slaves crossed via the path formed in the Red Sea and walked through as if they were on dry land. They were crossing the sea in an unheard-of way. They were truly living a miracle.

Fast approaching behind the fleeing Israelites was Pharaoh's army of battle chariots pulled by galloping horses. The pursuers were traveling at top speed to recapture their former slaves and return them to Egypt to continue building the largest empire of the time. Fear enveloped the children of Israel. They did not know that Someone who is above history was fighting for them. When the last Hebrew child's foot left the sea, the waters that had risen like walls closed up firmly, swallowing up Pharaoh's army within its waves.

The former slaves stood on the banks of freedom, amazed at what they had just experienced and seen. They could not believe the impossible that had just taken place. They saw the waves of the sea hitting the land, bringing with them the dead bodies of soldiers and horses. The chariots had a new resting place at the bottom of the sea. Hundreds of years of slavery were over for them and for their children. They started to scream and shout with shouts of victory. The enthusiasm began to flow through like a wave of energy from one person to the next, and suddenly, the three million began to sing. The Holy Ghost had united them in an enthusiasm they had never experienced before.

Miriam sang to them: "Sing to the LORD, for he is highly exalted. Both horse and driver he has hurled into the sea."[152]

The victory they experienced remained ingrained in the conscience of their people and, to this day, is still being passed from generation to generation.

Victories, whether personal or corporate, must remain like landmarks in people's conscience and history. Victories experienced because of God must be framed in the memory; their purpose is to develop faith and belief for future critical situations.

The Word of God and His interventions experienced in moments of crisis are pillars in the life of the believer that bring enthusiasm and courage when faced with other difficult stages in life. Too many people suffer from a sort of spiritual amnesia that manifests itself as forgetfulness of His interventions in past difficulties in life. *"May I never forget the good things he does for me."*[153]

Victories, whether personal or corporate, must remain like landmarks in people's conscience and history. They are the points of reference that you must resort to when faced with other crises.

From the banks of victory, the people headed through the desert toward the Promised Land. After three days of walking through the sweltering sun and the burning sand, they noticed that their water supplies had been exhausted. The young people, mothers, little children and elderly people had a difficult time dealing with the lack of water; after all, they were blazing a road they had never traveled before. No one had prepared them for anything like this journey. In the distance, the thirsty people saw the image of water, and they all rushed to it. Their first taste revealed the water was bitter and not drinkable. The water crisis became a problem that the thirsty people hit like a stone wall that kept them from moving forward, and they saw no viable solution.

Stopped at a place called Marah, facing the bitter waters, the three million people began to grumble against Moses. I wonder how that hum of three million people plotting in unison must have sounded? Three days prior they had lived a miraculous experience at the Red Sea and had felt on top of the world, but now they were facing a different matter and were living through a bitter experience.

And so it goes in life... You go through periods of victory when everything goes well, and then suddenly, you reach Marah and bitter water impossible to drink. Bitter water comes into our lives in different forms. Having a setback in business is a rest stop by some bitter waters. Losing someone dear brings a moment of sorrow. A divorce means passing through the town of Marah. When someone you trusted deceives you, you face life's bitter waters.

Suffering and sorrow come with something different for each of us. Even if the pain is universal, it knocks on each of our doors at different times, in different ways, and with differing levels of intensity.

If you glance at the map of your life, you will be able to identify such moments when you passed through times of sorrow. You never wanted to pass through there, but you reached that place. We do not know the future and do not know when we will have to pass through Marah, but we must understand that each problem has something hidden within it.

C. S. Lewis' *The Screwtape Letters* illustrates how a more experienced devil teaches a younger subordinate devil to deceive people. During that conversation, the mature devil teaches the other about the Law of Undulation[154] that people experience and how to use it to make them lose their way.

Simply stated, Lewis' Law of Undulation states that there are ups and downs as well as high points and low points in life. Such is the life that people live. The high points bring the false illusion that they will last forever, and the onset of bitter moments make them think that the normality of life has disappeared indefinitely. Believing that their state will not change creates disappointment and depression.

> As always, the first step is to keep knowledge out of his mind. Do not let him suspect the law of undulation. Let him assume that the first ardours of his conversion might have been expected to last, and ought to have lasted, forever, and that his present dryness is an equally permanent condition.[155]

Many people are not yet used to the fact that life has ups and downs, and the Devil uses this actuality to deceive them. I believe that we should use each problem or crisis to our advantage and understand the purpose for which God intended it.

The Bible contains 1,189 chapters, but each one is different. Likewise, life can be compared to a book with different chapters. At times you will feel like you are going through the chapters of tears with Jeremiah. Other times you feel like you

are in the victory chapter with David or perhaps in the tempta-
tion or joy chapters like Joseph. Do not judge a book or a life
by a single chapter because each chapter will only last a while
until another chapter or season of life begins.

Do not judge a book or a life by a single chapter,
and you must not judge a life by a single season.

Discover the Purpose

The town of Marah where they arrived was, in fact, a test,[156]
and this test revealed what was in their hearts. *"For whatever is
in your heart determines what you say."*[157]

The approximately three million people began to plot and
to show their reactions when facing the crisis. Their grumbling
was not caused by their circumstances; rather, their complain-
ing was a reaction of the heart and of their character when
faced with the pressing situation.

Moses was also facing the same crisis; however, his reaction was much different. He began to pray for a solution. What
a huge difference in their reactions! The attitude of the three
million people was the sign that God had to work on their
character.

Likewise, your encounter with the bitter waters of life will
reveal your spiritual maturity and whether your character still
needs work.

"Count it all joy when you fall into various trials, knowing that the testing of your faith produces patience. But let patience have its perfect work, that you may be perfect and complete, lacking nothing."[158]

The various trials, or bitter waters, you live through are like the olive press that holds you and compresses you, and their purpose is to make you become patient. This *trial-patience* process, in turn, has the purpose of perfecting you so that you may be more like Jesus. To be more like Him, you must go through the press of hardship to process you. If you look at the bitter waters through this lens of processing you into becoming closer to Jesus's character, trials begin to attain a new value.

Could it be possible that trials are, in fact, treasures?

Once, I was walking by the ocean with my wife Oana, and we saw a store that sold pearls. I went in and saw a display with a large selection of unique rings featuring luxurious pearls. An aquarium with live clams was visible near the window. I looked at the extraordinary pearls and again at the aquarium with clams and asked the store attendant, "Ma'am, what do you do with the clams?"

"In each clam in the water tank, a pearl is forming through the clam's suffering," she explained. "You choose a clam, and we will open it and make you a ring from that pearl."

That process was interesting to me. I questioned, "How do you know that the pearls in the clams are big enough to be put on rings?"

She explained that before the clams reached the water tank at the store, their specialist examined them through a device to check the size and value of the pearl. "If he felt any pearl needed more time inside the clam to get bigger, he would not put it up for sale. If he felt the pearl was ready to market, then we would bring it to the aquarium at the store."

While I looked at the pearls that adorned the rings, my mind wandered to the fact that each of us is a pearl in the making—a pearl formed through suffering and pain where no one can see. And the great Specialist—God—looks at each of us to see if we are ready to be displayed like the most valuable pearls. My friend, if you are under the pressure of God's workshop, do not get discouraged; you are in the process of becoming a valuable pearl.

If you are under the pressure of God's workshop, do not get discouraged, you are in the process of becoming a valuable pearl.

Discover the Solution

On the other hand, Moses, who was faced with the same bitter waters, had a different reaction. *"Moses cried out to the LORD..."*[159] He prayed for a solution to their problem; he didn't ask the people who were also powerless. Instead, he turned to God to show him a solution and to give him a way to resolve it.

"The LORD showed him a piece of wood. Moses threw it into the water, and this made the water good to drink."[160]

Biblicists have not yet reached a conclusion as to whether the piece of wood was lying on the shore or whether it was a tree that grew on the banks of the water. That wood had likely grown there or had been left there. The tree had possibly been planted years before by someone unknown or a seed had taken root in a crack in the ground and had grown. We do know that the wood, which was His solution to their problem, had been prepared by God before the children of Israel even reached the town of Marah. The solution was hidden from their eyes. From this point of view, the wood was a true treasure for them that was only revealed after prayer.

For the problems that you currently face or those that you will encounter in the future, He has already prepared solutions. These solutions are like treasures located in the spiritual dimension, but they are not visible with human eyes. You will have to fight through prayer to have them revealed and to see the solution is within the spiritual realm. God has already prepared the "piece of wood" that might sweeten your bitter situation, whether it be in the material, emotional, relational or any other area.

How many solutions to our pains are hidden to us because we only try to resolve them with our intellectual capacity and do not press to reveal them at the spiritual level? During prayer and fasting, the spiritual eyes of the soul open, and we begin to see what we could not see before. The loud life and overloaded schedule make us run and run, only to realize that we forget that time spent in His presence can reveal new plans and solutions that can lead us to resolving life's crises.

*During prayer and fasting, the spiritual eyes
of the soul open, and we begin to see
what we could not see before.*

Between the lines, Moses's reaction highlights a paradigm of spiritual man. What is it about? Man's life is like a priest's censer that needs coal and incense in order to work properly. The priest places burning coals in the censer and then he would put incense over the coals. The combination would result in a smoke that would change the smell in the atmosphere.

Trials are burning coals that burn in life's censer, and the incense is prayer. *"May my prayer be set before you like incense..."*[161] Putting the incense of prayer over the burning coals of trials will result in a smoke that will be a pleasant scent to God. The smoke resulting from this combination will help you see the solution to your problem in the spiritual dimension.

Those consumed by grumbling and plotting will not be able to see the solution in the spiritual realm. Grumbling blocks the eyes of the soul from seeing beyond the appearances of the material world. In the smoke of prayer, God's presence descends and brings the best ideas. These come when obstacles block our path, and God lights it with ideas and new options after prayer and revelations in the spiritual domain.

*The best ideas come when obstacles block our path,
and God lights it with new ideas and options
after prayer and revelations in the spiritual domain.*

The sweetening wood from Marah also speaks of a different wood that shall be revealed after thousands of years—the wood from the cross at Golgotha. When Jesus Christ was crucified on that cross of wood, He took on all of the sins and sorrows of humanity and became the solution for man to be free. The wood from Christ's cross reveals the solution that sweetens our lives. *"This message was kept secret for centuries and generations past, but now it has been revealed to God's people."*[162]

Discover HIM

After the miraculous solution to the crisis in Marah, God revealed an aspect about Himself that they did not know: *"I am the Lord, who heals you."*[163] That revelation remained ingrained in their minds, and in the hard moments in their lives, they were able to resort to *Jehovah-Rapha, the God who heals.*

Abraham went together with his son Isaac to offer a sacrifice on Mount Moriah. As they climbed the mountain, his son questioned, "Father, I see the wood, I see the fire. But where is the sacrifice?" This question simply tore the old father apart because God had asked him to bring his only son Isaac as a sacrifice. Old Abraham was going through such difficult times.

Abraham answered that God would take care of it. And,

indeed, God stopped Abraham from taking his son's life and showed him a ram with its horns stuck in some branches and told His servant that the ram was the sacrifice to offer. Therefore, *"Abraham called that place The LORD Will Provide."*[164] *Yehova Yire!*

God's revelation to man was gradual, and each experience remained ingrained like a truth that can be used in other episodes of life. We often have information and theories about Him that we have heard or that we've learned from others, but the best knowledge about Him is through the Bible and your own personal experience. Revelation and experience must be according to the Bible.

The Invisible Prison

Marah was only a test, but the sorrow that was felt throughout the test can come down quietly around man; it can take root, infect the soul and become an invisible prison for the soul. Tests were not created for the sprouts of sorrow to become a prison; nonetheless, many have been caught in it confines.

The next town that the Hebrews would come upon was not far. Some Biblicists speculate that Elim was only a distance of about 38 miles. Twelve freshwater springs, one for each tribe of Israel, were there as well as 70 palm trees where they could rest in the shade protected from the sun's rays. *Elim* meant "abundance, prosperity and blessing," but stopping at Marah and remaining in the prison of sorrow meant sabotaging God's plan to lead the people to blessing.

I've seen many people infected by the sorrow of a test who

no longer want to continue the path in the calling and plan that He destined for them. Their bitterness took root in their souls, and they no longer wanted to let it go.

What Do the Bitter Waters Mean?

Marah can mean that the test of sorrow is intended to reveal character and attitude traits that are not in Jesus's likeness and must be addressed. Marahs are a treasure because they help us become more like Him.

The bitter waters can be the way to discover the solution that He prepared that you had not seen. The solution can be discovered in the spiritual realm through prayer. Painful events can reveal aspects of God's character. Sometimes He allows bitter waters into our lives to bring us closer to Him.

Our episode with Edison, which I shared at the beginning of the book, was a bitter one for several months. I felt the oncoming storm would crush the boat of my life on the sharp rocks of bitterness for life. God helped me to survive that period victoriously because I poured out my prayer before Him. Both of my hands held tightly to the rope of faith and hope anchored to the throne of grace and mercy of God. The harder the waves hit, the tighter I gripped that rope of faith and hope.

Probably you are presently experiencing storms that will rise menacingly. Perhaps you have yet to experience these ominous storms. Whatever the case, I invite you to grasp with both hands the rope of faith and hope that is anchored by the throne of God. Pray insistently for Him to command the bitter storm to be silenced and to move away from your life and your family.

Reflection Group Questions

1. In what way does the Law of Undulation prepare us for moments of crisis?

2. If crises uncover negative spiritual attitudes in people's lives, how can crises be a blessing? How have you seen this manifested in your own life? What did you do to change this and continue to grow spiritually in a positive way?

3. Have you ever had an experience when, after praying to God, He revealed the solution to your crisis? How did you apply the trial-prayer paradigm?

4. How could you encourage someone who is facing an episode of sorrow and who no longer wants to follow the path of faith?

5. How can we discover aspects of God's character after resolving situations through His power?

Conclusion

Life is a journey that takes you on different paths. Some of them are a smooth and easy road that produce an abundance of joy. Instead, other paths are like wandering in the middle of a jungle without a compass and a map. There you feel your pounding heart ready to explode in your chest because you are no longer in control of the situation. You feel stalked by the eyes of the problems that are looking at you from behind the lines of events.

How will I get out of the jungle of trials and pains in which I get lost?

When will this complicated situation end?

Has God forgotten me here in my condition?

Why did the Great Designer allow this disease, weakness, or these things that put me in an inferior position?

When you look at life's journey from a human perspective, the questions that often knock on your mind can make you wander into the maze of unanswered thoughts and ideas. But when you look at it from God's perspective, you can see that even if you do not understand what is happening at the moment, you can still accept by faith based on His character and promises that He has a wonderful plan for your life.

Indeed, you will accept and probably understand some things now; others will make sense later in life after events connect with each other. You will never understand some events of life until you are with the Lord. Pray that the Heavenly Father will open the eyes of your heart to understand the role of things that are hard to accept in His divine plan.

Sometimes we feel like Elizabeth and Zechariah who felt abandoned to the pain of accusations and the fact that God does not answer prayers. But many have experienced that He works in the right time—as He raised the accusation of the old couple and miraculously answered their prayers, so He can do the same for us.

Onesimus crashed the car of his life on the most dangerous rollercoaster, but God took every shard and glued them together with His love. Later, the young Onesimus understood, as many of us understood, that God knows how to redeem any shipwreck in the mire of failures.

From Elijah's experience, we understand that thoughts build strong fortresses from which they lead human life. In the realm of the mind, a person cannot have both the fortress of victory and the fortress of victimization. The mind grinds on the thoughts you allow in, so instead put in the divine Word.

The road of disappointments is the busiest and most tramped-down road in the universe. Cleopas and his friend were walking on that road, but the scars of Jesus turned them back on the path of faith. In the same way, you must use your scars that once hurt you to turn those who walk the path of disappointments back to hope.

We often see ourselves in the mirror of Gideon's disadvantages. We see ourselves weak, helpless, and seemingly left behind, and we forget the disadvantages the Creator has allowed in our lives are the scene on which He works best. God is able to manifest His power and grace in a special way.

The display case with souvenirs that I took from my past experiences with the Lord is the most fertile ground in which faith grows. Those souvenirs forming the treasure of our faith must be guarded because the Evil One hangs around, seeking to destroy them.

Marah is the halt at the bitter waters of life. How many people do not reach the bitter waters where life becomes unbearable? For each bitterness God has prepared a solution; however, the final solution is the wood of the cross of Golgotha, which can sweeten any bitterness you experience.

One day you will understand why God allows certain things in your life. Remain in the faith that He has a wonderful plan for your life. Rely on His unchanging promises and character.

I would love to hear about your experience—how God transformed your incomprehensible situation into a trophy for His glory. You can write me about your experience at fromfailuretovictory@yahoo.com.

End Notes

Introduction
[1]2 Corinthians 12:9.
[2]2 Corinthians 4:7.

Chapter 1: Beyond Expectations
[3]Ephesians 3:20-21 (NIV).
[4]Luke 1:5-6, 8-9.
[5]Leo Tolstoy, *Anna Karenina* (Oxford, England: Oxford University Press, 2014), 3.
[6]Doug Greenwold, *Zechariah & Elizabeth. Persistent Faith in a Faithful God* (Rockville, Md.: Bible in Context Ministries, 2004), 21-22.
[7]Matthew 26:36 (ESV).
[8]Hillary Rodham Clinton, *Living History* (New York: Scribner, 2004), 236.
[9]2 Corinthians 12:8-9 (NIV).
[10]Psalm 139:16-17.
[11]Genesis 25:20-21, 26.
[12]Luke 1:13, 18-20 (NIV).
[13]Luke 1:18 (NIV).
[14]Isaiah 6:1b-3 (NIV).

[15]Luke 1:19-20 (NIV).
[16]Luke 1:24-25 (NIV).
[17]Galatians 4:4 (ESV).
[18]Ecclesiastes 3:1, 11 (ESV).
[19]Luke 1:34-37 (NIV).
[20]Luke 1:41 (NIV).

Chapter 2: In the Footsteps of a Fugitive

[21]Aristotle, *The Politics of Aristotle*, translated by B. Jowett (Oxford: The Clarendon Press, 1885) 6, https://www.stmarys-ca.edu/sites/default/files/attachments/files/Politics_1.pdf.

[22]Donald W. McCullough, *Waking from the American Dream: Growing Through Your Disappointments* (Downers Grove, Ill: InterVarsity Press, 1988), 122.

[23]Barbara Grizzuti Harrison, *The Astonishing World: Essays* (Boston: Ticknor & Fields,1992), 90.

[24]2 Samuel 18:5 (NLT).
[25]Galatians 6:7 (NLT).
[26]James 1:16-17 (NLT).

[27]Adapted from Laura E. Richards, "The Golden Windows," *Gateway to the Classics, 2005-2020*, http://www.gatewaytothe-classics.com/browse/display.php?author=richards&book=windows&story=golden.

[28]Dennis Rainey, *Pulling Weeds Planting Seeds: Growing Character in Your Life and Family* (LaVergne, Tenn.: Spring Arbor Distributors, 1989), 118.

[29]John 21:6 (NLT).
[30]John 21:7 (NLT).

[31]Genesis 37:28 (NIV).

[32]Thomas Mann, *Joseph and His Brothers*, trans. by H. T. Lowe-Porter (New York: Alfred A. Knopf Publishing, 1968), 447-48.

[33]Genesis 50:20 (ESV).

[34]Romans 8:28 (NIV).

[35]1 Peter 2:24 (NIV).

[36]Colossians 2:14 (NLT).

[37]2 Corinthians 5:21 (NJB).

[38]Brennan Manning. *The Ragamuffin Gospel: Good News for the Bedraggled, Beat-Up, and Burnt Out* (New York: The Crown Publishing Group, 2008), Kindle, 109.

[39]Fyodor Dostoyevsky, Crime and Punishment, trans. by Constance Garnett (New York: Random House, 1950), 322.

[40]1 John 1:9 (KJV).

[41]Philemon 17-20 (NLT).

[42]1 Timothy 2:5 (ESV).

[43]1 Timothy 2:5 (ESV)

[44]Luke 19:8b (NIV).

[45]Philemon 10-20 (NLT).

[46]Revelation 12:10

[47]2 Corinthians 5:21 (NIV).

[48]John R. Claypool, "Learning to Forgive Ourselves," in *Best Sermons 1*, ed. by James W. Cox (San Francisco: Harper & Row, 1988), 269.

Chapter 3: Beyond Expectations

[49]"How Vincenzo Peruggia Stole the Mona Lisa and Made it a Masterpiece," June 8, 2018, ATI, https://allthatsinteresting.com/vincenzo-peruggia-mona-lisa-theft.

[50]John 10:10 (ESV).

[51]1 Kings 17:1b (ESV).

[52]1 Kings 19:4 (ESV).

[53]John Milton, *Paradise Lost* (London: George Routledge and Sons, 1905), 15.

[54]Proverbs 4:23 (GNT).

[55]2 Corinthians 10:4-5 (NIV).

[56]The Editors of Encyclopædia Britannica, "Corinth, Greece," *britannica.com*, 2020, https://www.britannica.com/place/Corinth-Greece.

[57]Dr. Caroline Leaf, *Think, Learn, Succeed: Understanding and Using Your Mind to Thrive at School, the Workplace, and Life* (Ada, Mich.: Baker Publishing Group, 2018), Kindle Edition, 176.

[58]Jena E. Pincott, "Wicked Thoughts," *Psychology Today,* September 1, 2015, https://www.psychologytoday.com/us/articles/201509/wicked-thoughts.

[59]2 Corinthians 10:5b (NIV).

[60]Ephesians 6:16 (NIV).

[61]Isaiah 21:5 (NIV).

[62]1 Kings 19:7-8 (NIV).

[63]John 6:48, 51; 7:37.

[64]Romans 8:28 (ESV).

[65]Brené Brown, *Braving the Wilderness: The Quest for True*

Belonging and the Courage to Stand Alone (New York: Random House Publishing Group, 2017), Kindle Edition, 55.

[66]1 Kings 19:9-13 (ESV).

[67]2 Timothy 1:6-7.

[68]Hebrews 4:12 (NIV).

[69]John 8:31b-32 (NIV).

[70]1 Kings 19: 15-16 (ESV).

[71]1 Kings 19:16b (ESV).

[72]Proverbs 27:6 (NASB).

[73]Romans 12:2 (NIV).

Chapter 4: The Value of a Scar

[74]Blake Gopnik, "Golden Seams: The Japanese Art of Mending Ceramics at Freer, March 3, 2009, *Washington Post*, http://www.washingtonpost.com/wp-dyn/content/article/2009/03/02/AR2009030202723.html.

[75]Luke 24:21.

[76]Romans 8:28.

[77]Luke 22:31 (NLT).

[78]Psalm 139:16 (NIV).

[79]Ruth 1:20.

[80]Lysa TerKeurst, *It's Not Supposed to Be This Way: Finding Unexpected Strength When Disappointments Leave You Shattered* (Nashville: Thomas Nelson, 2018), Kindle Edition, 7.

[81]Psalm 34:8 (NIV).

[82]Luke 24:16 (NASB).

[82]Kendall, R.T. *When God Shows Up: How to Recognize the Unexpected Appearances of God in Your Life* (Lake Mary, Fla.:

Charisma House, 2008), Kindle Edition, 46.

[83]Luke 24:31 (NIV).

[84]Hal Donaldson, *Your Next 24 Hours: One Day of Kindness Can Change Everything* (Ada, Mich.: Baker Publishing Group, 2017), Kindle Edition, 15.

[85]Ibid.

[86]Ibid., 16.

[87]Luke 24:26-27 (NIV).

[88]John 20:25a (NIV).

[89]John 20:25b (NIV).

[91]Luke 24:32 (NLT).

[92]Genesis 50:20 (NLT).

Chapter 5: The Treasure Under the Ruins

[93]Hitler, Adolf. *Mein Kampf: English Translation of Mein Kamphf - Mein Kampt - Mein Kamphf* (p. 20). Kindle Edition; https://www.telegraph.co.uk/culture/art/art-news/7511134/Hitler-sketches-that-failed-to-secure-his-place-at-art-academy-to-be-auctioned.html.

[94]"Nazi Storage Sites for Art During World War II," *Wikipedia: The Free Encyclopedia,* 20 January 2020,https://en.wikipedia.org/wiki/Nazi_storage_sites_for_art_during_World_War_II.

[95]Godfrey Barker, "The Unfinished Art Business of World War Two," *BBC News,* 4 November 2013, https://www.bbc.com/news/world-europe-24812078.

[96]Judges 6-7.

[97]*Theodore Roosevelt, an Autobiography* (New York, Charles Scribner's Sons, 1922), 337.

[98]Jeff Lucas, *Gideon: Power from Weakness* (East Sussex, UK: Spring Harvest Publishing, 2004), 35.

[99]Ephesians 1:17-20 (NASB).

[100]Judges 6:14.

[101]Judges 6:15 (The Message)

[102]Mark 6:37 (TLB).

[103]John 6:5-6 (ESV).

[104]John 6:7 (BSB).

[105]Judges 6:15 (KJB).

[106]Psalm 68:5 (ESV).

[107]Judges 6:6:15 (NASB).

[108]Mark 2:22 (NIV).

[109]Judges 6:12, 14 (NIV).

[110]Priscilla Shirer, *Gideon: Your weakness. God's STRENGTH* (Nashville: LifeWay Press, 2013), 56.

[111]2 Corinthians 12:10 (NIV).

[112]2 Corinthians 4:7 (NIV).

[113]1 Corinthians 1:27 (ESV).

[114]Howard Taylor, *Hudson Taylor and the China Inland Mission: The Growth of a Work of God* (Irving W. Risch, 2015), Kindle Edition.

[115]Judges 6:21 (ESV).

[116]Judges 7:2 (NLT).

[117]Deuteronomy 20:8 (ESV)

[118]Lucas, *Gideon*, 131.

[119]Judges 7:2 (NLT).

[120]Judges 7:22 (NIV).

Chapter 6: Memories in the Display Case

[121]Joshua 4:6b (NIV).

[122]"God the healer."

[123]Vanessa Thorpe, "Magical Realism…and Fakery," *Guardian online*, 21 January 2001, https://www.theguardian.com/world/2001/jan/21/books.booksnews (accessed December 6, 2019).

[124]Ann Voskamp, *The Broken Way: A Daring Path into the Abundant Life* (Grand Rapids: Zondervan, 2016), Kindle, 35.

[125]2 Kings 20:1b (NIV).

[126]2 Kings 20:3 (NIV).

[127]2 Kings 20:5a-6a (NIV).

[128]Psalm 56:8, Revelation 7:17, 21:4.

[129]Philippians 4:6-7 (NIV).

[130]Isaiah 38:12, 14-16 (NIV).

[131]Judges 6:21.

[132]Habakkuk 2:2-3 (NASB).

[133]Erin Loechner, "The Story of Design," *Design for Mankind*, February 12, 2013, https://designformankind.com/2013/02/the-story-of-design/.

[134]2 Chronicles 32:31 (NLT).

[135]2 Chronicles 32:25 (NLT).

[136]Janet M. Hartley, Paul Keenan, Dominic Lieven, eds., *Russia and the Napoleonic Wars, in the War, Culture and Society, 1750 –1850* series (Palgrave Macmillan, UK 2015) Kindle, 191.

[137]Natasha Frost, "How the USSR Turned House of Worship Into Museums of Atheism," May 7, 2018, *Atlas Obscura*, https://www.atlasobscura.com/articles/soviet-antireligious-museums-of-atheism.

[138]Victoria Smolkin, *A Sacred Space Is Never Empty: A History of Soviet Atheism* (Princeton, N.J.: Princeton University Press, 2018), Kindle, 35.

[139]Judges 17:6b (ESV).

[140]Proverbs 22:6 (ESV).

[141]Elie Wiesel, *Night* (Night Trilogy) trans. by Marion Wiesel (New York: Farrar, Straus and Giroux, 2012), Kindle, 29.

[142]Wiesel, Elie. *Jew Today* (p. 18). Knopf Doubleday Publishing Group. Kindle Edition.

[143]Wiesel, *Jew Today,* 23.

[144]Proverbs 16:18 (ESV).

[145]2 Kings 20:15-17 (NLT).

[146]Judges 16:6 (NIV).

[147]2 Kings 20:17-19 (NLT).

Chapter 7: My Problem and My Solution

[148]Richard Pascale, Jerry Sternin, and Monique Sternin, *The Power of Positive Deviance: How Unlikely Innovators Solve the World's Toughest Problems* (Boston: Harvard Business Review Press, 2010), 23.

[149]Chip Heath and Dan heath, *Switch: How to Change Things When Change Is Hard* (New York: The Crown Publishing Group, 2010), Kindle, 29.

[150]Ibid., 32.

[151]2 Kings 6:17 (NIV).

[152]Exodus 15:21 (NIV).

[153]Psalm 103:2b (NLT).

[154]Lewis, C. S. *The Screwtape Letters* (San Francisco: HarperOne, 2009), Kindle, 37.

[155]Ibid., 45.

[156]Exodus 15:25.

[157]Matthew 12:34 (NLT).

[158]James 1:2-4 (NKJV).

[159]Exodus 15:25 (NIV).

[160]Exodus 15:25 (NLT).

[161]Psalm 141:2 (NIV).

[162]Colossians 1:26 (NLT).

[163]Exodus 15:26 (NIV).

[164]Genesis 22:14a (NIV).

End Notes

To my wife, Oana: you are truly my support!

To my son, Edison: you bring me happiness every day.

To my editor, Linda Stubblefield: your thoughtfulness to details made a big difference!

To my friends, Alina-Cristina Toma and Andreea Boscor: special thanks for your contribution.

Made in the USA
Columbia, SC
31 October 2020